W9-ABL-658

With the Author's love and
greetings to my dearest
Sisters of Carmel who
have always helped me

E. Boyd Barrett

Oct. 1952.

It was on the Feast of Our
Lady of Carmel that the
Publishers accepted this
book for publication

E Boyd Barrett.

LIFE BEGINS WITH LOVE

Life Begins With Love

BY

E. BOYD BARRETT

THE BRUCE PUBLISHING COMPANY
MILWAUKEE

Nihil obstat: JOHN A. SCHULIEN, S.T.D., Censor librorum
Imprimatur: ✠ MOYSES E. KILEY, Archiepiscopus Milwauchiensis
April 21, 1952

COPYRIGHT, 1952, THE BRUCE PUBLISHING COMPANY
MADE IN THE UNITED STATES OF AMERICA

PREFACE

THIS book is about love, its beauty, its worth, and its significance in life. It is written with deep conviction. It is a lesson learned after sitting on the school bench of life for threescore years. It is a lesson that others have learned, some quickly, some almost as slowly as I.

> "It took me all of fifty years,
> To reach this sure conclusion;
> There is no heaven but charity,
> No hell but in confusion" (W. B. Yeats).

The title of this book derives from St. John. It is not a mere daring slogan. It is, as it stands, revealed truth. Wrote St. John: "We know that we have passed from death to life because we love the brethren." With love comes life — the first days of life. LIFE BEGINS WITH LOVE.

People are unhappy who do not know love. They exist in darkness . . . in futility . . . in despair. "He that loveth not abideth in death" (St. John). People who know love are the happy ones. "He that loveth, flieth, runneth, rejoiceth; he is free and not bound" (À Kempis).

No one can have enough love in his heart; no one can love too much. Love is good through and through. "It worketh no evil" (St. Paul).

Love should be our highest ambition. It is *gold*, more precious than material gold. You give and give, but the more you give the more remains.

Love is a *cure-all;* the only cure-all. It heals the hearts of others and it heals your own heart.

Love, says À Kempis, is "the highest reason." Its insight is deeper than the intellect; its potency is greater than the will.

If I write of love it is because I feel particularly qualified to do so. I am qualified, not because my heart has ever been as it should be, warm and true — quite the contrary; but because I have been the recipient of unnumbered acts of kindness in word and deed and gift. I have experienced love. I have drunk deep and often of the life-giving ambrosia of human kindness. I look back on the road I have traveled and see a myriad of lights still aglimmer — lights that will never quite go out — for acts of brotherly love have a quality of immortality.

I am convinced of the reality of love. I *know* that there is a great amount of love in the world — much generosity, sympathy, forbearance, and noble graciousness, "without dissimulation."

Why do not people look upon acts of love so as to admire them as they admire flowers and the flight of birds? God draws forth wondrous beauty from nature; He draws forth even greater beauty from the human heart. What is fairer than the saying of a good word about another? Though you gild the lily, you can never gild an act of love. We crave for love; *our hearts crave to love.* Why do we imprison our hearts? Why not let them forth to love and serve our brothers?

O Holy Spirit, pour love into our hearts! *Infunde amorem cordibus!*

Though the story I have to tell is an old one, do not for that reason leave it unheard.

Peter, shortly before he was martyred, repeated his story of love in his Epistles. He knew that his followers had heard it often before but he warned them that he had "to put them in remembrance" so as "to stir them up."

The texts I quote and the thoughts I reword have undying value in them. Listen to them once again, so that you may renew yourselves in the spirit of love and begin the "life of love" afresh.

CONTENTS

LIFE BEGINS WITH LOVE

Chapter 1

WHAT IS LOVE?

MANY think of love as a tender fondness or as a generous pity, but true love goes far beyond sentiment and feeling. It is of the mind and the will and the hand, as well as of the heart. There is action and substance in it, rather than warmth and sound. It is "in deed and truth," not "in word and on the tongue. . . ." The heart that has love in it is "kind, merciful, forgiving"; it is "a right heart." It is "to love" that St. Paul exhorts us when he says: "Whilst we have time let us work good to all men."

True love is a very *real* action that commands our respect. When we witness it we admire it spontaneously as a most admirable thing. Often it amazes us, leaving us speechless with wonder!

One time I was living in a Jesuit college when a fire broke out at night. The college was situated in the country and there was no fire-fighting equipment within miles. The flames spread rapidly and enveloped an attic and the wooden stairway leading up to it. A servant boy was asleep (or unconscious) in the attic. We all knew the boy. His name was Tom.

As we looked on, the flames grew fiercer. Billows of smoke poured out of the passage leading to the stairway. We heard the crackling of burning wood. It seemed that nothing could be done to save the boy. We were on the threshold of tragedy.

Then a man joined the onlookers. He was a big, slow-moving, pale-faced man. He was Brother James, the college cook, a retiring type of religious, who was known to spend a great part of his time praying in the college chapel.

Brother James gazed thoughtfully at the smoke and flames. He saw and heard what we saw and heard, but he did not think what we others thought, that nothing could be done to save the servant boy, Tom.

With his head down, Brother James suddenly dashed into the fire. We heard his heavy footfalls on the burning stairs. There followed a long pause and the fire seemed to grow in intensity. Brother James was in the attic now, wrapping blankets about the boy and taking him in his arms. Also, no doubt, he was saying a last prayer.

Again we heard the heavy pounding of descending footfalls. Brother James at last appeared, coming through the black smoke, his soutane ablaze. The boy was in his arms and he carried him to a safe place before he collapsed.

We who were mere onlookers didn't say a word. Our hearts were bursting with emotion, thrilled, overawed, by the amazing thing we had witnessed.

The *thing* that moved us, the thing Brother James had done was *an act of love*. To call it heroism is to employ a meaningless term. It was great love, rather than great heroism, that the humble lay Brother revealed.

Stories come to us these days from Korea that tell of acts of love that eclipse in grandeur the tale I have just related. We hear, for example, of a young American sergeant, John A. Pitman, who readily embraced the certainty of death when he threw himself on a live grenade to save his men by smothering the explosion. By a miracle he survived. We read too of the pilot of a helicopter who made a descent into enemy territory, amid a hail of shells and bullets, to pick up a fellow pilot whose plane had crashed.

Some of us, without further thought, take for granted such acts as things that happen in war — heroic deeds. But unless we analyze the nature of these acts, probing into them until we come to the human heart, we shall never understand the incredible beauty of love.

In a little book, with which readers are no doubt familiar, *The Imitation of Christ*, there is a description of love that is graphic and daring and true. À Kempis, shrewd and clear-witted, had great and varied experience of human and divine love and it moved him to write:

"Love . . . is a great and thorough good. . . . It equalizes every inequality. . . . It will not be kept back by anything low or mean. . . . It feels no burden. . . . It thinks nothing of trouble. . . . It attempts what is above its strength. . . . It pleads no excuse of impossibility. . . . Though weary it is not tired. . . . Though alarmed it is not confounded. . . . Than it there is nothing more courageous, nothing higher. . . . He that loveth, flieth, runneth, rejoiceth; he is free and not bound."

Were one to ask me directly: "What is love?" I would answer thus, basing my answer on things that I have seen or known:

"Love is a young soldier at the front, scared and miserable, who writes a cheerful letter home to his parents. Love is a man who promises to find a job for an unfortunate misfit and keeps his promise. Love is a woman who, on discovering another woman's shameful secret, does not reveal it. Love is a thrifty housewife who takes the best she has in her icebox to lay before an unwanted guest, and serves him with style on her best table linen. Love is a college boy who learns the deaf alphabet in order to converse with a lonely old lady who cannot hear. Love is the one who gives abundantly and gives gladly when a beggar returns to ask another alms. Love is the person who, instead of recriminating, sees his own shortcomings in another's faults. Love is the grateful soul who remembers his indebtedness and repays as best he can."

There is no pretense, no make-believe in love. It is, as St. Paul said, "without dissimulation." The three words St. Peter uses of love, "earnest . . . sincere . . . brotherly," indicate its character of genuineness. Whereas sentimental impulses and emotions lead to danger when they wax violent, love can never be too strong or too intense. It is "born of God" (À Kempis) and it "worketh no evil" (St. Paul). The more love there is in the human heart, the better; is not the world's most devastating famine the dearth of love?

What is our attitude toward love? Why have we not more confidence in its value and its grandeur?

We place various ambitions before the young. We encourage them to become great scholars, great artists and musicians, great athletes, and so forth. We encourage them to aim high, to cultivate their minds, their sense of beauty, their spirit of adventure or of research. We bid them develop every body organ from the eye to the ear, from the brain to the hand; and every human faculty from running and thinking to singing — with one sole exception. We forget or neglect to encourage them to employ their hearts — to love.

Is there no teacher to say, or better, no father to say: "Look, Son. Would you aim high? Very high? Well, the greatest ambition that a man can have is to possess a good heart, 'a right heart,' a heart with real love in it. No matter what happens to your head or your arms, take care that nothing hardens or chills your heart. With a heart full of kindness toward your fellow men, you will be happy and you will make others happy. Let that be your ambition. What more do you want in life?"

Gandhi, the Indian seer, knew the noble call in love when he said: "If a single man achieves the highest kind of love it will be sufficient to neutralize the hate of millions."

There was a popular writer who maintained that life begins at forty, and it may be that a more mature life does begin at about that age. It may be that a fuller life begins when we "find ourselves" and commence to realize our ambitions. For many, a happier domestic life begins with an ideal marriage and the founding of a family. But it is only when the human heart learns to beat in brotherly harmony with one's fellows, when the dictates of true charity are obeyed, that the life we were created to live begins.

Life begins with love because love implies escape from slavery to the ego and from fears that beset and darken our days. "Fear is not in charity, but perfect charity casteth out fear" (St. John).

Life begins with love because it enhances our abilities and perfects us. "Love enlarges all the powers of the soul" (À Kempis).

Life begins with love because it makes true democrats and brothers of us. "Love equalizes every inequality" (À Kempis).

As I quote these words, "love equalizes every inequality," there comes back the memory of a gifted young doctor, whose way it was to take seriously the counsel, "go and do likewise," that appends the Gospel story of the Good Samaritan.

It was a cold and rainy afternoon in winter when he stood looking out the window of his residence-office on a bleak square of Dublin City. As he stood there he saw a man passing in threadbare clothes and broken shoes. The man was coughing violently as he stumbled slowly through the puddles of the pathway, pulling his thin coat about him.

Here was a victim of circumstances, wounded and friendless on a highway, in as hard a plight as the one the Good Samaritan had helped. "I've a spare coat and shoes for that brother of mine," the young doctor thought, as he tapped on his office window and signed to the wayfarer that he wanted him.

He opened his office door and brought the stranger inside. He made him put on the warm overcoat and the shoes he had for him. He made him sit down to rest and warm himself at the fire, while he got food and something for him to drink. And when his guest was rested and refreshed he gave him money to help him on his way.

There was no trace of "inequality" in the way the doctor did these things; there was no questioning or counseling or "talking down" to him; there was no forced effort "to uplift" his visitor; there was only the easy, humble way of kindliness and love.

From where, we ask ourselves, does this wonderful thing, love, come? Does it grow of itself in the heart from seed planted by God? Must it be cultivated? Are there rules governing its development? If so, what are they?

"Tell boys and girls," wrote Dr. Albert Schweitzer, "that the truths they feel deep down in their hearts are the real truths. God's love speaks to us in our hearts and tries to work through us in the world."

There is propaganda for love and brotherhood these days. Many are the calls for more tolerance, more amity among men and nations, more sacrifice. There is genuine indignation when, day after day, new social wounds and sores are revealed and publicized. There is horror at the

graft and peculation rampant in high places; at the sordid
corruption of the young by peddlers of dope; at the crime
and robbery bound up with gambling rackets. Well-
intentioned men demand quick action to cure the ills of
hate and greed, thinking, foolishly, that masses of evil-
doers can be cured *en masse*.

But thoughtful men know that reforms can only be accomplished as the result of individual effort. Each one
must save his own soul. Each one must learn for himself
what love is, and each one must learn to love at a personal
cost. There is no quick cure for social wrong. Least of all
can mass cures be looked for, as though greed and hate,
like physical maladies, could be banished by innoculations.

The bringing into vogue of love and brotherhood need
not, however, be quite as slow and hopeless as might
seem at first thought. When the individual begins his life
anew and travels "the excellent way," he influences others.
Love is infectious. When we see another who is kind and
honest, we, of necessity, become less unkind, less dishonest. The great lover is a wonderful fellow, a stirring
example for all. His love, says À Kempis, is "active, sincere, affectionate, pleasant, and amiable; courageous, patient, faithful, prudent, long-suffering, manly, and never
seeking self." Long-sighted and wise, À Kempis did not
dream of underselling the power of love. He summed up
his optimism in six pregnant words: "He does much who
loves much."

Love has to do with *all* our human contacts. Love finds
an opportunity when the phone bell rings; when a door
is left open; when a stranger jostles you on the street;

when an inquiry is made to you about a person; when some kind of help is needed; even when a stray dog looks up at you in helpless doubt. The opportunities for love are ubiquitous — love never has a moment to rest.

Poor distracted love! Called hither and thither; besought by this one and that; doubted, derided, often puzzled; bravely hopeful even in failure; but "feeling no burden, thinking nothing of trouble, pleading no excuse; though weary, never tired" (À Kempis). Is there any limit to what love is asked to do or to give? Must love not be ready even "to lay down life for the brethren"?

The test of love is action. To love is to do something good and it springs into being in the will. Effusive cordiality, eye-laden pity, the caress of warm affection, a sympathetic wish — these fall far short of the reality that is love. "If a brother or sister be naked and want daily food; and if one of you say to them: 'Go in peace! Be you warmed and filled!' yet give them not those things that are necessary for the body, what shall it profit?" (St. James.) What a mockery words of pity and sympathy can be on your lips when you lock your hands *and do nothing!*

Dr. Schweitzer asked us to make brotherhood "our second job," a kind of hobby, but that is not enough. Brotherhood should be our way of life, our main highway, and not a mere hobby or pastime. On this road of love, self comes second, "each one considering not the things that are his own, but those that are other men's" (St. Paul). The road is passable, full of romance and adventure, and it is not lonely, for many, happily, travel that way. There are no dark shadows or gloom, for "he that loveth his brother abideth in the light." God's protection is over the travelers. "Do not forget to do good and to impart; for by such sacrifices God's favor is obtained" (St. Paul).

The meaning of love and brotherhood, its beauty, its inspiration, can be told best by means of a story. The story need not be about one of the famous philanthropists or one of the great saints; it suffices to glance at the life of a simple, unknown nun.

One time, many years ago, I visited a home for the aged poor in the great Belgian city of Liège. It was a large institution conducted by Sisters of the Poor, and it was supported by voluntary subscriptions. Most of the inmates were quite destitute; most, also, were sick and decrepit. The work of the Sisters was difficult and exhausting, and as often happens in such institutions it was understaffed. As I passed from ward to ward, I saw the Sisters going about their trying work, busy and cheerful, and my heart melted in pity for them as well as for the wretched people they attended.

In one ward I stood for a moment beside the bed of an irritable old man whom a little Sister was endeavoring to pacify. I said something in French to the Sister. At once her hands stopped smoothing the old man's pillow. She seemed almost breathless for a second — as though she saw a vision — then there was a flicker of her eyelids and the beginning of a wondrously happy smile.

"Are you from Ireland?" Sister asked in English.

"I am," I said.

"Praise be to God! You're the first I've seen in twenty years. And how is Ireland?"

I told her all the news about our country and she in turn told me how she had left Galway as a young girl to join the Sisters of the Poor in Belgium. She had come to work in the strange, lonely city of Liège, and "had never seen a soul from Ireland" since. She told me how happy she had been "doing" for God's poor, though she often thought of home and longed to see some of her own countrymen.

Her eyes filled with tears but she brushed them away — and smiled again.

We chatted until a bell rang and we said, "Good-by — *Dhia agus Muire duit*" — in Irish. Perhaps Sister never again saw "a soul from Ireland," but the love that was in her heart was strong enough to sustain her and keep her happy. Hers was a great love — and she had no fears at all. "Perfect charity casteth out fear" (St. Paul).

Chapter 2

THE NEED OF LOVE

THE greatest discovery is the discovery of the obvious, the discovery of some plain fact that people see *without seeing*. Such a plain fact is the need of love.

Father Damien saw this need; and Frederick Ozanam and John Bosco and Mother Cabrini — and thousands of others from Florence Nightingale to Albert Schweitzer and Father Flanagan of Boys Town.

Meanwhile thousands of others never make the discovery that without love we cannot deal with the situations that confront us in life. Have we grasped — do we understand — that the equipment we need most to lead good and happy lives is love?

We can make our discovery of the need of love in various ways. Some saw Volga boatmen hauling barges; some saw tenants driven from their homes on Irish hillsides; some saw famine-stricken Indian children; and with such sights came the realization that the world needs love. Albert Schweitzer, the German musician and scholar, saw in his mind's eye disease-ridden African natives and conceived a bright vision of "the fellowship of those who bear the mark of pain," who "know the horrors of suffering to which man can be exposed."

14

Humans longing to be free from pain — and such humans exist everywhere — prove the need of love.

Dr. Schweitzer voiced what we all should understand in our hearts as well as in our heads, when he said: "What the world lacks most today is men who occupy themselves with the needs of others."

A little boy may have a mother who is beautiful, gay, generous, and good, and he may be very fond of her. He may say to her often: "Mother, I love you!" And he may *feel* the sweet, sincere affection that his words denote. But he will still be very far from any sense of "the need of love" of which I am speaking.

If his good, gay mother is wise — as my mother was — she will introduce her boy into some grim reality of life and put him face to face with penury and suffering.

If she brings him, for example, to visit a poor widow who is old and sick and very lonely and who is dependent on others for any brightness that she may have in life, the boy will have a chance of grasping what "the need of love" means.

If he begins to put aside a dime or two out of his pocket money for the poor widow, and to bring her a share of a box of candy that he is given for a present, he will, and perhaps for the first time, experience real love . . . and, with love, *religion*. "Religion clean and undefiled before God . . . to visit . . . widows in their tribulations" (St. James).

Unless a boy comes to understand "the need of love," his life will be a long and dreary walk "in darkness," and he will search in vain for peace.

In Dickens' *Christmas Carol*, the well-known story of Mr. Scrooge is a case in point. Scrooge's life was harsh and unhappy until, thanks to his famous dream, it came home to him what he lacked was love. What a change resulted! Dickens might well have anticipated me and entitled his story of Scrooge: LIFE BEGINS WITH LOVE.

In present-day propaganda for love and brotherhood it is often implied that the need of amity among men and nations is due to the great red revolution that is afoot. But love and brotherhood are needed, not on account of threatening upheavals, but on account of the perennial suffering and distress of man in his sojourn here below. Some suffer from physical ailments; some from hunger and want; the others, the rest of us without exception, are poor in one respect or another. We all need aid — we all need love. "The poor you have always with you," said Christ to His Apostles. And until the end of time there will be work aplenty for kind, compassionate hearts.

Look around at the intolerance, hate, suspicion, thieving, and crime that is rife — man fighting his fellow man. Men should not hate one another as they do, nor should they despise one another's rights. Men should be conscious of their common humanity, and of their adoption by God as His children. Men should know that they are brothers in virtue of this adoption . . . and being brothers they should learn to love. What is missing in man's heart is love. Man's greatest need is love. St. Paul knew this when he prayed: "May the Lord make you abound in charity towards one another, and towards all men."

With the development of benevolence in government, such as is experienced in this country, and with the rapid expansion of institutional charity, some may be inclined to excuse themselves from social activities on the ground that "everything is taken care of by experts." Men subscribe generously to deserving charities and take a holiday from serving their fellow men, saying: "Now I have done my share. My quota of brotherhood is met."

The man who gives generously and in the right spirit to deserving charity is a splendid fellow. What he has done is immortal; its effects will never die. But good and great though his act may be, it does not meet his quota of love. It is only a beginning, or another step along the road. The more love does, the more it urges itself on to other acts. Though all the blind and all the lame and diseased and poverty-stricken in the world were taken care of by institutional charities, there would still remain a vast mass of suffering and grief uncared for. The largest class of sufferers are those who can only be helped by individual sympathy and guidance and care. There is never a moment (save when you are alone) that there is not someone within reach of your voice whose heart can be helped by your love if your love is true.

Love takes on various forms according to situations and circumstances. What, for instance, does love require of the member of a family or community? What shape or form does it assume? We know that love is sorely needed in family and community life. We know that laborsaving gadgets, and gadgets designed to entertain, cannot make up for the absence of love. Neither furnishings nor wealth and plenty can convert a house into a home, unless the spirit of love is there.

Some rich houses are like morgues; some are like bedlams; only those where kindness and patience and understanding dwell are *homes*.

What does love say to the member of a family or a community? First of all, "Be generous." "Give to him who asketh of thee and from him who would borrow of thee turn not away" (St. Matthew).

Love says, through the lips of St. Paul: "Bear with one another and forgive one another, if any have a complaint against another, even as the Lord hath forgiven you, do you also"; "rebuke not the aged"; "lie not one to another"; "provoke not the young to indignation lest they be discouraged."

A home needs love in the form of generosity, patience, truthfulness, and mutual kindness.

Outside the home, in business dealings and social life, love assumes other forms. There is one form of such paramount importance that it claims special mention.

There is a human need that we all feel, which transcends all other needs. It is commoner and more widespread than the need of food or shelter or other material help. It is the need we feel of being treated with respect; of being recognized as an equal, on the basis of our humanity; of having our fundamental rights recognized. However ignorant and poor a man may be, however low he may have fallen either morally or socially, he still craves for respect. It is the part of love to satisfy this human need, and unless we do so neither our minds nor our hearts are right.

St. Peter, in three immortal words, lays down the law: "Honor all men." And he makes no exceptions. With like splendid understanding of the duty of love, St. Paul tells us: "Love one another with the charity of brotherhood, with honor preventing one another."

In social and business life, then — as well, of course, as in home life — love takes on the form of honoring and respecting others — all others. Never is it right to despise or belittle a fellow man. "Who art thou that judgest thy brother?" (St. Paul.)

For harmony and peace in living; for spreading and increasing human happiness, there is a never ending need of showing respect and honor, and that is love.

Oscar Wilde, ruined and disgraced, as he stood on the railway platform awaiting transportation to a term in Reading Jail, tells beautifully and emotionally of being "honored" by a dignified gentleman who lifted his hat to him in respect. There was love in that act and it was the act of a Christian.

Peter Claver, with his arms around a dying Negro, amid the stench and filth of the hold of a slave ship, is another of many possible pictures that illustrate Peter's law of love, "Honor all men."

In the depths of our own hearts we find ourselves incomplete, dependent, craving for understanding and sympathy. We should not be ashamed of this apparent weakness, nor should we be so foolish as to deny its existence. In Christ, the Perfect One, a yearning for sympathy was present. In His Agony did He not beg His Apostles "to watch one hour" with Him? We cannot stand alone. We are never self-sufficient. We look to others for our happiness. Whether we do so openly or covertly, we are, all the time, calling for help.

Full well we all know the need of love. A hundred times each day we experience it.

The blessed discovery that some make is the corollary to this fact of personal knowledge — namely, that others also need help and love, that they need our help and the love that we can give them. If we are dependent upon others for our happiness, they, in turn, are dependent upon us for their happiness.

What we seek from others we can render to them.

What we seek is respect, an honest deal, kindliness, and understanding — things that others should and could easily accord us. Love prompts us to give to others the things that we need from them; namely, to honor them, to be honest in our dealings with them, and to be kind and understanding toward them.

Such is the program of love in broad outline.

At times the need of love is felt poignantly and manifested under tragic circumstances.

I had a friend, a scholar of Yale University, who enlisted in the French Red Cross soon after the outbreak of World War I. He was sent to the front with an ambulance corps to collect the wounded.

One day, after a battle, he went into a field looking

for casualties, and came upon a German boy who was dying.

My friend was rabidly anti-German, a "Hun-hater," but this boy's plight moved him.

The wounded boy looked up at him beseechingly and said in broken English that he wanted a little favor. His request was that my friend sit by his side and hold his hand.

My friend sat down and put his arm about the boy and listened while he told about his mother and his home, and how he wanted word to be sent to his mother that he was thinking of her as he was dying.

My friend promised this request and, with his arm still around the boy's shoulders, comforted him as well as he could. He felt, he told me later, as though his own brother were dying. He stayed on to the end — knowing that that was what the poor lad needed.

Such is brotherhood — such is love.

God wants us to act in that way.

Chapter 3

THE SECRET OF BROTHERHOOD

SOMETIMES we do what we mean to be an act of kindness to someone. We do it with sympathy and generosity; it may be at no small cost to ourselves. Our intention is good; our purpose is to be of help. And yet we find, to our dismay, that we hurt rather than please. Our kind act is a failure.

Apparently there was something wrong in the way we did our deed of brotherliness. What was it? What is the "blind spot" in our charity?

À Kempis, wise as well as idealistic about love, warns us that "many seek their own ends in what they do, yet know it not." Like all of us, À Kempis had experience of favors done him, gifts bestowed upon him, advice given him, *in the wrong way*. He reflected and prayed over his personal experiences, and finally discovered "the secret of brotherhood," which he reveals in the pages of *The Imitation*.

In the Gospel we find salutary hints about the ways in which love should and should not act. We are told not "to sound a trumpet" when we do a good deed, and we are told not "to let the left hand know what the right hand does." Charity should, in a way, be utterly *noiseless*

22

— it should be so quiet and unobtrusive that even the hand is not seen to move, nor the lips to stir. When we draw attention to our kind deeds and seek for admiration, we are not acting through love but through pride.

Some, if asked the question, "What is the secret of brotherhood?" would reply: "Generosity. To give freely and give in full measure is the main thing in brotherhood." Others would offer a different answer, saying: "Sympathy and understanding are the essential elements of brotherhood." Still others might answer: "Self-sacrifice is the hallmark of true brotherhood. When you put your neighbor's need before your own you are manifesting true love."

However, none of these answers is correct. Although generosity, sympathy, and self-sacrifice are ingredients of true charity, they are not enough. Many a man is generous, sympathetic, and self-sacrificing, yet lacking in the most important character of brotherhood. He may still hurt very much the one he seeks to help — he may still make an enemy instead of a friend out of his beneficiary.

What is the way to give in order that your gift to another may be acceptable? What quality must you have to forgive freely and fully? In order to respect and honor all men, what kind must you be? If it be your duty to advise or reprimand others, what virtue do you need to fulfill such duties without doing harm? What temper of mind and heart must you possess to refrain from judging others? And from showing intolerance? What disposition must be yours to yield to your neighbor the right of way, and the best share of what is going, for love's sake?

There is one and the same answer to all these questions — and that answer indicates the first essential of
true brotherhood.

The answer is humility — a modest, just estimate of oneself — and of one's own unimportance.

Humility is the secret, the prerequisite, the essential
characteristic of true brotherhood.

St. Paul, one of the greatest, as well as the most loving
of men, warned us: "Let nothing be done through vain-
glory, but in humility let each esteem others as better
than himself."

À Kempis amplifies this teaching in these words: "If
thou hast any good believe that others have more . . .
it is no harm to thee if thou place thyself below all
others; but it is great harm to thee if thou place thyself
above even one."

Deeds of love and brotherhood fail when they are done
in an arrogant, superior, or condescending way. Deeds of
love done with any show of pride, or with any evidence
of conferring a favor, hurt more than they help. And, to
return to the opening paragraph of this chapter, when
we find that one of our well-intentioned acts of kindness
proves "a flop," we should look for the reason in our own
conceit. It is personal vanity that is the blind spot in
our charity.

The world looks askance at humility. The world ap-
proves the man or woman who is full of self-assurance,
and who asserts his or her rights with an air of authority.
The world listens tolerantly to big claims and big boasts
and often defers to arrant impostors. Meanwhile the man

or woman who prefers to be modest and retiring rather than self-assertive and clamorous, is looked upon as a case for a psychiatrist.

The worldly mind is, of course, too uninformed, and too obtuse, to appreciate the truth and beauty of humility. The worldly mind is unable to grasp the meaning of À Kempis' famous dictum: "That is the highest and most profitable lesson when a man truly knoweth and judgeth lowly of himself."

It requires a fine mind and an honest mind to understand and admit with À Kempis that "he who knoweth himself well is vile in his own eyes." And it requires faith and love to embrace humility as a necessary virtue in the new life, "the excellent way," of brotherhood.

Readers will still be puzzled over the connection between humility and charity. They will continue to say to themselves: "But surely, I can be kind and obliging to my neighbors, generous in my giving, and careful not to discuss others' faults, without being possessed of this virtue, humility."

In answer to this objection, I think it will be found that the would-be good neighbor, who despises humility, insists on doing things in his own way. He is prone to find fault with the opinions of others and to prefer his own. He is self-opinionated and difficult. His vanity leads to disagreements and quarrels. He overvalues his own wisdom and experience. He criticizes, and his judgments (even though not outwardly voiced) are unfair and partial. He is bound to be intolerant — self-righteous. He does not, as À Kempis advises, "guard against and subdue

those faults that displease in others," for the reason that
he sees no faults in himself.

The vain man is blind — and a blind man cannot do
much to help others.

If a man thinks that he can give an alms in the right
way without the grace of humility he is deceiving himself.

Speaking from experience, as one who has been many
times the recipient of alms, I think that it requires a
great deal of true humility to give an alms in a way that
is sweet and painless to the recipient. Not often is an
alms given that is an all-around blessing, "that blesses
him who gives and him who receives." Delicacy and tact
in the manner of giving spring only from a humble heart.

If only benefactors realized the hurt and shame that
their crude (or proud) manner of giving causes!

St. James in a striking story gives us a distressing
picture of tactlessness in dealing with a poor man. He
calls it "dishonoring the poor man," and it is quite clear
that he felt very angry about it. "If," he writes, "there
shall come into your assembly a man having a golden ring,
in fine apparel, and there shall come in also a poor man
in mean attire, and you have respect to him that is clothed
with the fine apparel, and shall say to him: 'Sit thou here
well (comfortably)!' but say to the poor man: 'Stand
thou there!' or 'Sit under my footstool!' do you not judge
within yourselves and become judges of unjust thoughts?'"

In contrast to such a proud and tactless way of acting,
we have the way of the meek and humble of heart, the
true Franciscans of life. They are gentle and unobtrusive
in the way they do things. They act in a modest, un-

assuming way. They leave themselves out of what they are doing; they are not boastful or importunate. They cause no pain. When they give they make it appear that the thing they give is not really theirs but yours. They convey to you, or remind you, that "what they have they have received." They are not purse-proud, for in their humility they admit that God is the Giver of all things; that of themselves they have nothing.

As a nation, we Americans are not conspicuous for humility. We give freely and generously to other peoples, but we are prone to boast of our benefactions. Sometimes we hurt and antagonize other nations by our boastings. We proclaim ourselves to be "the great moral leaders of the world," "the greatest (and richest) nation on earth"; but in so doing we provoke bitter criticisms of our obvious shortcomings. Peoples react like individuals and only appreciate benevolence when it is garbed in lowliness.

The connection between brotherhood and humility is so important that we must stress it further.

As long as we maintain an inflated idea of our own importance, as long as we prefer ourselves to others, we live a false, unreal life. Our true life, our worth-while life, begins only when we deflate ourselves and prefer others. Then we can love others and be loved by them.

As long as we remain proud and arrogant others dislike us and distrust us, for they see we are guided by false notions. We are still ignorant of "the highest and most important lesson," that (to requote À Kempis) of "truly knowing and judging lowly of oneself."

The close connection between charity and personal

modesty is brought out by À Kempis' four rules (*Imitation*, Bk. III, Chap. XXIII). These four rules, which he calls "the way of peace and of true liberty," are at one and the same time rules of brotherhood and rules of humility. They are:

I. Do the will of another rather than thine own.
II. Choose always to have less rather than more.
III. Seek always the lowest place and to be beneath everyone.
IV. Wish and pray that the will of God be fulfilled in thee.

These are the rules of true brotherhood. The kind-hearted man defers to the wishes of others; he allows others to have the best places and the nicest things; he stays in the background yielding the publicity to those who seek it; and, of course, he aims at fulfilling his duty to God by loving his neighbor.

In a life of love, self comes second and the neighbor comes first.

The rules are rules of humility, for they run counter to the conduct of the proud man who wants the best of everything as his right, and who wants the first place and his own way.

There is, no doubt, high virtue involved in obeying À Kempis' four rules, but the man who obeys them "enters the borders of peace and rest." He has the exquisite satisfaction of leading a life of love.

The connection between humility and charity is not mere theory; the monk, À Kempis, himself lived what he wrote. Indeed he lost his job as *Economiae Praefectus* of his convent through being "overkind" to the poor. And there are others — who is there that does not know of one? The one who is kind because he is humble, and humble because he is kind?

I knew one at college long ago, a Father John, a gifted little man, who was the "Mr. Fix-it" for the boys. All their broken watches, ice skates, bicycles, and gadgets passed through his hands for repair; and he never grumbled much or refused anyone. Despite being a great physicist, and the best teacher on the staff, he was at the beck and call of every selfish ragamuffin in the school. Always there was a grin on his face and he knew every boy by his first name.

He never talked piety to the boys or paraded his own. But it was curious that, when confession time came around on Saturday nights, all the "hard cases" crowded his confessional.

No one dreads telling sins to a priest who is very humble and very obliging. No "handout," be it material or spiritual, from a modest, loving heart, hurts or offends.

Chapter 4

THE PROFIT IN BROTHERHOOD

THE greatest act of brotherhood is a spiritual one. It is to be present at Mass; to be present, that is, with sympathy and love at the deathbed of Christ. In that act, says an old Irish proverb, there is "great gain." In other lesser acts of brotherhood, there is likewise great gain, both spiritual and temporal. Love enriches man in many ways.

We do not seek pecuniary recompense for brotherly services, nor do we seek fame. The man with love in his heart hides from view, as far as he can, the kind deeds he does. Nevertheless, it is peculiar to brotherhood to be its own reward. All that you do for others comes back to you in some form. What is given in charity is lent to God, and such loans are repaid with ample interest. There is truth in the inscription that Joseph Addison found on an old tombstone in England: "What I spent, I lost; what I possessed is left to others; what I gave away remains to me."

There is first of all a sense of satisfaction that is quite different from vain complacency, when we help others in their troubles. We feel that we have accomplished something worth while. If it is only to spend an hour or two reading for a blind man, or to secure free hospitalization for a member of a poor family, a brotherly deed changes the nature of your day from a wasteful to a profitable one. You feel that the day was worth living. You feel happier.

Among the natural rewards that the practice of brotherhood brings in its wake, there are three which deserve special attention. First, culture and development of the mind; second, mental health and self-control; third (though not always), the love and gratitude of others.

First, as regards culture and development of the mind. As love of others prompts us to be unfailingly courteous and considerate we grow in refinement. Through thinking about the needs of others, what they want, what we can do for them, we see and understand things better; our minds are exercised and developed. As À Kempis said: "Love enlarges all the powers of the soul."

The kind man is, in the best sense, a "civilized" man. There is none of the crudity and greed of egocentrism in him. He does not grab the best place, the largest share, nor whine if he does not have his way. He makes way for others and is glad to do so. "You first, please!" is in his heart as well as on his lips.

Thanks to his preoccupation about the interests of others, the kind man gains in memory and imagination. Being truly tolerant, he sees both sides and his judgment improves. He is spared the confusion and darkness of prejudice and bigotry. His horizons widen. As one writer, Karl Deschweinitz, puts it: "To him who strives to understand his fellows and their problems, life begins to reveal itself in deepening richness and wonder. The old fears, the old prejudices disappear, leaving him free to receive the truth." While charity "fulfills the law," it also improves man's mental stature and his temperament.

As a second gain in brotherhood, we find mental health and self-control.

The source of many mental and moral maladies, and a factor in every neurosis, is excessive preoccupation about self. Men fret and worry over their health, their selfish interests, their real or imaginary fears. They "eat their hearts out" in concern over themselves. They multiply their miseries by directing their thoughts inward. Their ego becomes a vulture that preys upon them, literally tearing them to pieces. In such condition their one hope is to escape — to escape from the vulture — their own ego.

How many would be saved from sheer misery, from the tyranny of fear, if they switched their thoughts from self to others, and took up brotherhood even as a hobby!

Sometimes a great personal sorrow brings about an excess of self-pity, a brooding melancholy; in this introversive state the best — and, I think, the only — remedy lies in taking up a work of charity.

There was a fireman in New York City, retired and childless, who was suddenly and violently bereaved by his wife's death. All his life he had depended upon her, and now that she was gone he fell into deep gloom. He lost all interest in life and spent his days brooding over his fate. All he could think of, to shake off his near-despair, was to jump into his car and drive at breakneck speed, as in the old days he had driven his fire truck.

Then there came to his ear a call for help. One of his

nieces fell ill of an incurable disease and was confined to a city institution. The old fireman was asked to go to see her. Making a great effort, he went. The patient begged him to come again. Once more he visited her. Soon his visits became a habit. He began to bring the poor girl flowers and presents. Then he obtained permission to bring her out for drives in his car. Unconsciously a new interest in life awakened. By his devotion to another, by his brotherhood, his life regained meaning. He had found an escape from his neurotic self-pity. The therapy of Christian love had saved him.

Brotherhood will save, or help save us, as well from the tyranny of passion as from the tyranny of morbid fear. People who are slaves of passion, victims for example of the alcohol habit, can more easily regain self-control if they devote themselves earnestly to the service of others. Gluttony, anger, jealousy, unchastity, as well as other passions, are forms of morbid self-love. They represent sinful indulgence of the ego. According as men interest themselves *in doing things for others,* they lessen the dominance of their passions. They regain, in part at least, their grip on the helm that guides their lives. Their will grows stronger. Charity, as St. Paul said, "envieth not . . . seeketh not her own . . . is not provoked to anger . . . rejoiceth not in evil." Charity is the enemy of passion.

The third reward that accrues to the practice of brotherhood is somewhat uncertain, but when it comes it is sweet and consoling. I refer to love and gratitude.

We do not give ourselves to others by way of service

in order to win their affection and their thanks. Our motive is to please God. Nonetheless, when humans appreciate our efforts on their behalf, and show their appreciation, we cannot help being very happy.

Gratitude is a fine and rare virtue, and when it is shown one understands how a good deed "blesses him that gives and him that receives." Gratitude is at times stupendous, outlasting decades, outdistancing oceans, defying even pain and death.

One time this writer was of service to a young woman in helping her by psychiatric advice to overcome a light neurosis. Years passed; he forgot about the case. Then one day, a quarter of a century later, he received a letter from her, from the other side of the world, telling how she had always remembered him and how "not one day had passed in all those years that she had not offered her prayers at Mass for him."

Gratitude is such a touching and beautiful thing (when we ourselves experience it), it is strange that we are so negligent and indifferent about showing it.

Once while living on the Aran Isles, bleak rocky acres lying in the Atlantic, west of Galway, I had been of help to the family of a fisherman. He was, besides being very poor, a shy fellow — but, as I was to discover, "his heart was right"; he was grateful for what I had done.

When it came time for me to leave the islands I went aboard the *Dun Aengus,* a very small packet boat, that lay offshore. The sea was choppy and it was an adventure being carried out to the ship in one of those canvas shells that are called *currachs.*

The *Dun Aengus* had begun to move out to sea when I saw, as I stood at the rail, a *currach,* manned by one man, approaching swiftly. The man in the boat was the shy fisherman whose family I had helped. He came close to my ship, looked up and saw me, and then took from the bottom of his *currach* a large, live lobster and handed it up to me with a smile. "May your road rise up with you!" he said in Irish, as he smiled and rowed away.

In that live lobster in my hand I saw a big and loving reward for a little kindness. And was I happy!

There are still other gains in brotherhood that are wonderfully consoling, but not so easy to describe. There is the happiness of seeing how love makes love to grow; how others, seeing you do a kind thing, imitate and surpass your efforts. There is the joy of winning over to friendship one who hates and despises you. There is, above all, the ecstasy of winning a soul to God through dint of loving efforts. "He," says St. James, "who causeth a sinner to be converted from the error of his way, shall save his soul from death and shall cover a multitude of sins."

And now a story comes to me that illustrates very strikingly the gain there is in brotherhood.

A short while ago, a poor woman whom I knew was in a hospital in Rochester. Half her body was in casts; she endured continuous agony.

One day a Catholic nurse told her of another patient, a dying woman, who was in terrible trouble of mind because her husband was a non-Catholic and "bitter." She feared he would not bring up their children in the faith when she was gone.

My friend, the woman in casts, immediately sent a message to the dying woman that she was offering all her sufferings for her and her children.

The sequel to this fine act of brotherhood is almost unbelievable. Within a few days, the husband of the dying woman, the "bitter" non-Catholic, called to see my friend to tell her how moved he had been by her charity, and how he had resolved to become a Catholic before his wife died.

Chapter 5

THE CHOICE LOVE MAKES

No ONE can force you to love others. If you prefer, you can decline to be concerned about them. You can cultivate your own interests exclusively, leaving others to look out for themselves. You can refuse to help them in their troubles. You can refuse alms to the needy and deny protection to those who are in danger. In adopting this "self first" philosophy, or in persevering in it if it has always been your philosophy, you act with great worldly prudence. And if you are cunning you need not let others know that your heart is cold and sour. You can assume a veneer of kindliness when people are watching you, and so you will escape the opprobrium that belongs to a selfish man.

The philosophy of "self first" will save you from a hundred and one troublesome demands upon your time and your pocketbook. It will spare you the tedium of listening to tales of woe, and the exhaustion of expending sympathy. It will keep you from becoming involved in situations where sacrifice might be demanded of you. Above all, it will restrain you from acting in the incredibly "foolish" way that characterizes men who love their neighbors.

For, beyond a doubt, there is a quality of folly and madness in brotherhood. Kind men are always more than a little "crazy."

When you allow love to dominate your heart you lose common sense, the "practical sense." You give when you can't afford to give; you work without seeking or getting a cent of payment for what you do. You find food and rest for others, though you yourself are hungrier and more tired than they. You allow others to have the best places and the largest portions and content yourself with a poor place and a small share. Your philosophy is not "self first" but "self second." You play the fool.

The man who, driving along a highway intent on business, stops his car and then goes to fetch gas for folk in a stalled car, though no unusual hero, exemplifies the philosophy of love. He concerns himself about his neighbors' troubles, and puts their needs before his own. The boy who picks up a stray dog and, without thinking of getting a reward, carries it to the pound where its owners can recover it, acts with a like instinct of neighborliness. There is much wonder and beauty — as well as folly — in such acts of brotherhood.

The great choice that love is called on to make is a reorientation of our thoughts and actions from self-service to the service of others. There are calls on love at every hour in the small happenings, the commonplace events, of daily living. Every occasion on which it is possible for us to be courteous, obliging, helpful is such a call. Every time the doorbell or the phone bell rings our good will and charity are put to the test. We can be affable, or we can be cold and curt. We can humiliate another, or we can make another a little happier.

When someone stops you on the street to ask for a direction, it is one thing to give the answer sourly in terms of left and right turns; it is another, a better thing, to walk to the corner with the stranger and point out plainly and graciously the street or building he is looking for. When someone admires the blooms in your garden and asks for one, it is one thing to pick a couple that are not so good and hand them to your visitor; it is another, a better thing, to pick a big bunch of your very best and tie them neatly so that they may easily be carried. When we give we should give the best we have. That is the instinct of love.

There are people who are good neighbors through natural benevolence, without any conscious motive of a supernatural kind. Their good deeds are done in a spiritual mist. They are lovable, praiseworthy, and no doubt very dear to God. There are others, and they are to be imitated, who have a strong impelling motive in their charity that is definitely supernatural. Their good deeds are not done in the mist or in darkness for they "follow Christ." All they do for others is done directly or indirectly for Christ. They see Christ in every friend, neighbor, or stranger; they love every friend, neighbor, or stranger in Christ. Their faith adds depth and strength to their love. For them it comes easy to be kind and to love. They are tender toward morons, cripples, sinners, for they recall Christ's words: "What you do to the least of these My little ones you do unto Me."

The call of love, as we have said before, is for the most part to perform trivial acts of service. But at times there comes a call to face great danger for another's sake. Most of us, at one time or another, have witnessed heroic deeds. Let me recount a few personal experiences, as one's own memories come easiest to the pen. They illustrate "the choice that love makes."

Once, on a stormy day, I went down to a swimming place called "The Forty Foot Hole," at a rocky point, south of Dublin. When I arrived I saw a group of people watching a gallant rescue. One young man was pulling another ashore through the rocks and waves. Both of them were badly cut and bleeding from the buffeting. The rescuer seemed exhausted but he struggled hard, holding on to the other's body and keeping his head above water. He was not a trained rescuer but he was a hero. At last he got him ashore.

When it was all over I stood nearby watching the rescued man. His eyes were fixed on the other's face. He was looking at a stranger who had risked his life to save him. I heard him saying over and over again: "You're a good man! You're a good man!" Everyone there, looking on and listening as I was, knew that what he said was true. On that day, long years ago, love uttered a call and the call was answered.

How are we going to answer when love makes a sudden — and perhaps unwelcome — call upon us?

We pick up our mail in the morning and among the letters we find one in a handwriting that is vaguely familiar. As we read down the closely written pages our heart sinks. It is a tale of woe and winds up with a piteous appeal for help. We remember the writer, and his character is not above suspicion. His trouble is obviously real, but what can we do?

The appeal comes at a time when we ourselves are hard pressed for money; when things look "blue"; when disappointments are numerous. We feel in no mood to help anyone; we are "fed up." Still love has made a call upon us. In our hearts there is a cry — barely audible. "Can't you at least do something for this poor fellow?"

The moment has come either to harden our heart and tear up the begging letter, or to reach for pen, paper, and checkbook, saying to ourselves: "I'm going to write as kind a letter as I can because it's a letter to Christ!"

If you cannot do everything (or anywhere near to everything) that a beggar asks of you, do something at least, something decent and generous — something that shows you honor and respect him.

You are at home — or in your office — and someone comes to see you. You know your visitor — years ago, in better days, he was an equal and a friend. But he is sadly changed from those days.

He is "seedy" looking; his clothes are worn; his appearance shocks you — you think that he has been drinking — his face is red and pimply. Besides, as he stands before you, you notice that he is apologetic and ashamed.

He sits down at your request. He pours out his hard-luck story. He tells you, in so many words, that he is at the end of his tether. He has no money to pay for his room; he has no prospect of getting a job; he needs clothes and shoes; he hasn't had a decent meal in weeks.

As you listen you inwardly bewail your lot that you should be the target of broken-down bums. You'd like to get rid of the fellow at once, even though he was a friend — or acquaintance — in the past. You revolt against the situation — against being subjected to such annoyance.

Take care!

Your heart is losing temperature!

If it freezes through and through, you will be dead!

Look at this man again as he sits, sobbing, in your chair. Whether you like him or not, he is your brother. Whether it be his own fault or not, his need is real.

Perhaps it is beyond your power to find a job for him, or to supply him with new clothes; but at least you can do something for him. He has to have food and shelter, a few things in a handbag, and a little money. It is within your power to give or lend him a temporary respite from his suffering.

Listen to the cry in the depth of your heart: "Can't you do something for this poor fellow?" Close your eyes for a moment and remind yourself that he is Christ.

If we are to save our lives we must lose them — we must be forever giving them away to others. That is the choice that love makes — and it is a blessed choice.

Chapter 6

FIDELITY

When you break a promise, you bruise and hurt a heart; you may even break it. When you go through life, as many do, making and breaking promises, you leave suffering and gall in your wake. Until you realize that faithlessness in promises is the antithesis of brotherhood; until you realize that our country needs, above all else, honest men who keep their word, you cannot live a worth-while social life. Fidelity is active good will toward others; fidelity is love.

When I was a little fellow I learned the meaning of a broken promise. I learned it the hard way.

I wanted a drum, a big drum, and I wanted it badly. I thought I'd be very happy banging away all day with drumsticks in my fists. I hoped against hope that someone would give me a drum.

Then, one day, a cousin came to see me. She was very pretty and she was rich. She asked me what I would like and I said: "I want a drum!" She smiled and promised to send me a nice drum. My heart jumped for joy, I felt so happy.

From then on I could think of nothing but of the grand drum I was going to get. Every morning I ran

43

down the street to meet the mailman to see if he had my drum. The days passed and it did not come, but I knew in the depths of my little heart that it would come all right because my cousin — Emmy was her name — had certainly promised it to me.

Weeks went by and months — no drum! I was very sad that it hadn't come but I still expected it. A year passed — no drum! Even then I didn't give up hope. It wasn't until I was no longer a little fellow who could enjoy a drum that I finally began to forget about it. It was too late then. I no longer wanted a drum. But, how I had suffered!

I had been deceived, humiliated, hurt, disillusioned. My cousin, by her false promise, had dealt me a cruel blow; had darkened my young life quite a little. Why had she ever made that promise? Why, having made it, did she not keep it? Why had she lied to me? Why had she robbed me of a bright hope?

To break a promise to a child may seem to be a trivial thing and utterly unimportant, but here is the same kind of injustice and cruelty in breaking a promise to a child as there is in breaking the more serious promises that are made to adults.

A man is out of a job. He looks for one everywhere but fails to find one. He is in sore distress. A long time passes and he grows discouraged. His appearance deteriorates; he begins to look "seedy." He comes to you in his trouble and you promise to do something for him, to get him a job.

Now, hope awakens in him. He trusts you, and his happiness is dependent upon what you do. It means everything to him that you keep your promise. But you let him down! You say to yourself, "Oh, I can't be bothered!" You forget about him.

Why did you make that promise? Why did you increase the poor man's sorrow by awakening false hope? Why were you so cruel? So unjust?

Many people read the New Testament without noticing the emphasis that is laid upon telling the truth and being honest in human relations. The Apostles make it clear that fidelity is of the essence of brotherhood and love. "Lie not to one another," St. Paul says; and he repeats: "Putting away lying, speak ye the truth, every man with his neighbor, for we are members of one another." He condemns "the double-tongued," just as St. James condemns "the double-minded," saying: "A double-minded man is inconstant in all his ways." The breaker of promises is both double-tongued and double-minded. There is no love in his heart.

Fidelity in undertakings is a rare virtue. There are thousands who are temperate; thousands who are chaste; thousands who are generous and brave; but how few are impeccable in respect to the promises they make!

Who amongst us is not aghast, bewildered, angered, when he looks back over the years, and recalls to mind the promises that have been made to him and never kept? Thousands of promises! Whether solicited or unsolicited, whether by relatives or friends, whether about important or trivial matters, whether by word of mouth or in writing, these promises were made only to be broken. Among all the people whom we know, of how many can we say: "He is a man who *always* keeps his word"?

There are such, however — men who always keep their word. When they promise to meet you somewhere, hail, rain, or snow, they turn up — and punctually. Like the horseman who brought "The Good News from Ghent," nothing but death can stop them from keeping their promises. They are the kind of friends that it is precious to have. They are not double-tongued or double-minded. You can trust them.

There was a boy I knew in New York City, whose name was Tom. He used to bring me parcels from the laundry; and he was always punctual, a quiet, business-like lad.

One day he told me that if he could get his fare to Texas he could get trained as a mechanic. "If you can help me out I'll pay you back," he said. Without even knowing his second name I lent him the money.

A few years later Tom returned to New York, and the first thing he did was to call on me and return the sum I had given him. There was a glint in his eye as he repaid me. I saw he found happiness in being "a man of his word."

It is interesting to note how St. Paul takes time off in his Epistle to the Philippians, to tell the story of the magnificent fidelity of Epaphroditus, whom he calls "my brother, and fellow laborer, and fellow-soldier," and how he calls on the Philippians to "treat him with honor."

Epaphroditus had been commissioned by the Philippians to carry a gift to Paul, and he risked his life in doing so, "for indeed he was sick, nigh unto death." Paul says: "Because for the work of Christ he came to the point of death, delivering his life, that he might fulfill that which on your part was wanting towards my service."

Paul was deeply grateful for the gift so loyally delivered. "I have all and abound; I am filled, having received from Epaphroditus the things you sent, an odor of sweetness, an acceptable sacrifice pleasing to God. And may God supply all your want!"

People who are indifferent to what they promise, and in consequence lax about fulfilling their promises, are unlikely to be honest in their business lives. They cultivate the faculty of deception and lose self-respect. Soon they begin to tread the path of slick and tricky trading. It is only a matter of degree between them and cheats and swindlers. Consciously and unconsciously they fool others with their false promises. For them St. Paul has a sharp word: "Let no man over-reach or circumvent his brother in business, because the Lord is the avenger of all these things."

In this connection, namely, the evil habit of "over-reaching" in business, St. James thunders against the rich in a well-known passage: "Behold the hire of the laborers, who have reaped down your fields, which by fraud has been kept back by you, crieth; and the cry of them hath entered into the ears of the Lord of Sabaoth."

Apart from the ill and suffering that broken promises bring upon families and individuals, they constitute the greatest social evil, and the gravest danger of the nation. Infidelity in marital life, leading to divorce; infidelity in public office, leading to peculation and loss of confidence in government; and infidelity in business contracts, large and small, constitute America's greatest menace. Threats of war come and pass. Usually a big army and a pyramid of armaments take care of the danger of war. The safety of the nation is only momentarily involved in an international crisis. But the moral sickness of cheating, lying, and faithlessness in business and government and home life, that is so widespread and so continuous, saps the nation's strength and takes away her safety. America's greatest need is not for soldiers or guns, but for men who respect their pledged oaths, who keep their promises.

It is up to every good Christian, every loyal citizen, and everyone who wants to help and serve his fellow men, to learn and practice the virtue of keeping his promises.

Is it possible for a man to acquire this virtue of fidelity? I think it is not only possible but, for most, relatively easy. It calls only for the formation of a new and better habit, for a little self-control, for a little exercise of strength of will. Prayer, too, is of course necessary — the prayer to the Holy Spirit: *"Infunde amorem cordibus"* — "Pour *love* into our hearts!" For fidelity is deep and abiding love of others. Fidelity is "honoring all men."

When a man wants to put himself straight in the matter of his promises there is a preliminary duty he should attend to. First he should take a sheet of paper or a notebook and write down, one by one, all the promises he has made that he has not so far fulfilled. If he search his memory faithfully he will discover a great number of them, large and small. Those that are not in his power to fulfill, he should cancel. Those that are in his power to fulfill he should attend to without delay.

Having thus "wiped the slate clean," he should face the future with a new outlook on the virtue of fidelity, determining to be, in future, "a man of his word." Henceforth he should make few promises, and only such as are well within his power to keep.

Always it is unwise to make vague or ill-defined promises. A promise should be definite and conditioned. For example, if you promise to try to find work for a man, tell him simply and honestly that you will approach two or three employers whom you know and put his case before them — but that you can do no more. If there is any more that you can do, do it by all means, but don't promise.

There are men who promise to pay their pastor ten dollars a month toward the new parish building. After a month or two they default. It would be better for them to promise only five or three dollars a month and pay that sum faithfully.

Make few promises. Mean them when you make them. And when you have made them let nothing hinder your fulfilling them. People will respect you and rely on you; people will trust you if there is that kind of truth and fidelity in your heart.

If you would love your neighbor, rather than deceive him; if you would develop the very essence of brotherhood; if you would be a true friend of people in sorrow; if you would be a worth-while citizen, the first rule you must observe is that of keeping your promises.

Chapter 7

TOLERANCE

RACIAL tolerance is a good thing, and rare. It means that a man respects and admires people of every race and color. It means that a man has no bias against any nation and that he is completely free of the nationalistic hates that trouble the world. For such a one, in St. Paul's words, "there is neither Gentile nor Jew; circumcision nor uncircumcision; Barbarian nor Scythian; bond nor free; but Christ is all and in all." Racial tolerance, in everyday life, means that a man welcomes the company of an Indian or a Chinaman as much as of a fellow countryman, and that he stands opposed to any form of discrimination based on color or blood.

Religious tolerance is likewise a good thing, and rare. It means that a man respects and admires people of all religious beliefs. While a man should be convinced of the truth of his own religion, he should at the same time concede to everyone the right to follow his own religious convictions, and take it for granted that members of religions other than his own are "in good faith." Religious tolerance means that a man eschews that "bitter zeal" which the Apostle James says is not "wisdom descending from above but earthly, sensual, devilish." While the tolerant man repudiates the sophism that "one religion is as good as another," he sees in every religion an effort to worship God, and rejoices in that effort. In his daily life, he likes and lives at peace with "heretical" neighbors, honoring them and respecting them.

But though racial and religious tolerance are excellent as far as they go, they are not enough. They only touch the fringe of true and universal tolerance.

There is a fundamental tolerance, the most important tolerance of all, which consists of "forbearance," of making allowance for the faults and deficiencies of others, and of avoiding judging and condemning others. St. Paul, the archetype of tolerance, expounds it thus: "But thou, why judgest thou thy brother? Or thou, why dost thou despise thy brother? For we shall all stand before the judgment seat of Christ."

This tolerance of forbearance means that we live happily and contentedly with others who differ from us in their ways and in their opinions, and who are even antipathic to us. It means that we fully recognize the right of others to form their own likes and their own views and to maintain them without interference from us. It means that, far from despising others on account of their ignorance, their conceit, their mistakes, their uncouth manners, their ill temper, we deal with them patiently and kindly, "bearing with one another, and forgiving one another if any man have a complaint against another. Even as the Lord hath forgiven you, so do you also" (St. Paul).

There are many who cry out against religious and

racial bias and who strive manfully with voice and pen to put an end to oppression and persecution, but who still lack that essential tolerance which implies avoiding harsh and hasty judgments. There is gall and bitterness in the things they say and write. These public advocates of tolerance by their pride and violence belie true tolerance. To be truly tolerant one has to be humble and patient, understanding one's own frailty and shortcomings, as well as the frailty and shortcomings of others. It is not part of a truly tolerant man to exaggerate or misrepresent the faults of those whom he accuses of intolerance.

If we choose brotherhood as our way of life, we need to understand and practice tolerance. We have to learn to live amicably with people who have faults that are hard to put up with. Nay more, we have to learn to like such people and to serve them as devotedly as others who are easy to get on with. We have to ground ourselves well in the principles of tolerance.

First of all we must fully and freely accord to others the rights that we justly claim for ourselves.

The tolerant man hears another voicing an opinion with which he disagrees. Instead of getting angry and excited; instead of preparing arguments to refute the other, he should listen with interest and respect. He should say to himself: "Well, he has the right to form his own judgment on this matter. He may be right and I may be quite wrong, as I often am. Let me try to get his point of view clearly — I may learn something I didn't know from him."

The intolerant man, on hearing an opinion with which

he disagrees, shows displeasure and hostility. Assuming himself to be better informed than the other, he starts to argue — often without allowing the other to expound his point of view fully. He sets out to correct the other, to put the other right, and often he grows hot and angry. Quarrels arise in this way; and no good comes out of the discussion. St. Paul, no doubt speaking from experience, warns us: "Contend not in words for it is to no profit"; and again: "Avoid foolish questions, and genealogies and contentions and strivings about the law. For they are unprofitable and vain."

If you enjoy an argument — think of the other fellow as well as yourself — make it a pleasure for him by remaining good-tempered and broad-minded. Never try to *force* your opinion on the other. Always remember that even though your opinion *may* be the correct one, your proof or argument may be all wrong.

A second broad principle of tolerance is that we must "take things as they come." In other words, we must gladly accept all that Providence ordains.

We find ourselves thrown among "difficult" or "unpleasant" people — we have to live with them — we cannot change them — we must, therefore, "make the most of them," as they are.

Here we have the great problem of tolerance. Here we have a problem much more difficult, and indeed much more important, than the problem of racial or religious tolerance. Here we have the great test of the love that is in a man's heart.

The difficult, the unpleasant one may be the boss in an

office, the foreman in the gang, a fellow teacher on a school staff, a relative who lives in the same house, or just a close neighbor. The difficult or unpleasant one may be mean, bad-tempered, rude, deceitful, lazy, insolent, interfering, boastful, discontented, and may dislike you heartily. Nonetheless, you have to honor and respect such a one and live on friendly terms with him — seizing occasions to be of assistance to him in a kindly way.

If you lack patience and humility you will adopt the wrong attitude and say: "I can't stand him! I hate his guts!"

If, on the other hand, you have patience and humility, and faith in the power of love, you will say: "I'm going to like him! I'm going to treat him as a brother!"

The crux of the problem of tolerance is, then, how to like an unlikable person, how to accept him and cherish him as a brother.

We must face this everyday task with confidence because success is possible. No doubt we must exercise a little coercion on ourselves to avoid being discourteous or unfriendly. We need a little self-control to keep cool and cheerful under the annoyances and irritations that the other causes. We must refuse to take offense at what the other says or does, reminding ourselves that others have to put up with our own annoying manners. We set ourselves to take an interest in the unpleasant person and to seek out occasions of being obliging to him. We think about his needs, his troubles, his difficulties, and help to make things easy for him. Often with a little patience and understanding we can turn odious characters into good friends.

When others make mistakes through ignorance or clumsiness, instead of getting angry we should call to mind that we make plenty of mistakes ourselves. It is intolerant on our part to show pained surprise over another's error.

One day I left an advertisement in a newspaper office and the girl who took my copy glanced over it. I happened to know that she was a college girl; her manner was somewhat superior. With her pencil she changed the spelling of the word *sure*, which occurred in my copy, to *shure*. My tolerance failed me. Instead of letting the matter pass in silence I stammered an excited protest.

Sometimes we imagine we are being very tolerant when, in reality, our conduct reveals silly snobbery.

I had a letter once from a very liberal Protestant parson in which he told me about an apostolic Catholic priest in his town. He wrote: "My wife and I have him to dinner sometimes. We like him very much in spite of his table manners."

When we say of someone that we like him "in spite of" something, we are not being tolerant although we think we are. We are making a reservation. It is of that quality about which we make the reservation that we should be tolerant. We say, for example: "So-and-so is all right, *but* he talks too loud." Why carp at the fact that So-and-so talks in a loud voice? It may be a habit that he has acquired for a very good reason. There may be a lot of deafness in his family.

Our prejudices are the cause of much of our intolerance. We have many prejudices, some easy to detect, others latent. It is important for us to make ourselves clearly conscious of all these prejudices that hamper and blind us. An obvious way is to take the trouble to introspect a little and then *write out a list of our unreasoned likes and dislikes* — the people, the groups, the popular opinions that we abhor. Behind most of these antipathies we shall find *an inexplicable blind feeling*. Such blind feelings are a weakness, a disgrace to a civilized mind; they are prejudices that should be gotten rid of.

I confess to my shame that for a long time, well into my adult years, I was under the influence of that ugly blind feeling known as anti-Semitism. Without any good reason I was antagonistic to all Jews. This feeling did not derive from my education or from my religion. I fail to trace its origin. Somehow I slipped into thinking of Jews as nasty schemers who were lacking in courage and honesty. I had had a few unhappy business deals with Jews — as indeed I had had with Christians — and a sullen morosity against Jews developed.

Then, rather suddenly, I became ashamed of my groundless *feeling*. I came to recognize that Jews gave me my faith; that Jews launched and established, under God's providence, the Catholic Church. I took to heart the fact that Christ's nearest and dearest were all Jews. I came to see all that the world owes in art, science, scholarship, and idealism to this great, supreme race. I recognized at last the sufferings, wanderings, and heroic fortitude of the Jews — their eternal youth. I came to rejoice when great and noble members of my Church proclaimed their honor and respect for the Jewish race. In fine, as if it were overnight, I was delivered from a shameful and besetting intolerance; love and sincere regard replaced dislike. I need not say that my second state of mind was happier than the first.

When we conquer one intolerance we go on to conquer others. As an Irishman, who suffered in some degree from the old-time tyranny of the English Government, and who had a long memory for the wrong done to Ireland by England, I hated the English race. This hate in my heart was almost fanatical. I rejoiced when wars, from the Boer War on, hurt England's power and prestige. Mine was a blind and bitter intolerance. "God strike the English down!" was my prayer.

Then, thanks to some unknown grace, I faced and studied this ugly feeling in my mind. I saw that a man must forgive his enemies, make allowances for wrongs done, and replace hate with brotherliness. I reflected that in the long and sad course of English-Irish relations there were wrongs on both sides, good men and bad on both sides, misunderstandings on both sides. Now the past was past, and it was right that amity and respect should replace ill will. Once more, a shameful, senseless antagonism faded from my heart, and I felt the sweetness of finding another tolerance.

In tolerance we should aim high; we should aim at getting rid of every antipathy. "Loving one another with the charity of brotherhood, with honor preventing one another . . . if it be possible as much as is in you having peace with all men" (St. Paul). I think it greatly lessens a man's stature when he hates or despises any individual or any race. It is harder to honor and respect an intolerant man than any other.

If fidelity be the first rule of brotherhood, tolerance is the second.

Chapter 8

LOVE MEANS "THE GOOD WORD"

THERE is a quality that endears a man to us, and makes us respect him; it is the quality of always having "the good word" on his lips.

His greeting is affable; his welcome is cordial and sincere; he is plentiful in his praise and generous in his thanks; he expresses his appreciation for what you do, courteously; he has a "soft answer" to disarm you in an argument; he is never sarcastic, nor does he ever utter a sneer; a word of sympathy from him rings true; he belittles no one, nor judges anyone; he lives up to the old adage: "If you can't say a good word about a person, don't say a bad one."

Such a person does not blame you or utter recriminations if you make a mess of things. At most he murmurs: "There's nothing bad but could be worse!"

The man with the good word has a clean and wholesome tongue that smells of honey. He is one of the rare great, with no limit to the goodness of his heart. "He is truly great who hath great love" (À Kempis).

It is a truism that we are all prone to believe and speak evil of others rather than good, but few of us are conscious of this unhappy propensity. We do not realize that our tongues are dangerous; that they are, as St. James says, "unquiet evils full of deadly poison." Were we wise we would prefer to keep silent rather than to talk. But, as À Kempis tells us, "The most part of men are given to talk too much and therefore little trust is to be placed in them." Our folly in gabbing undermines our credit.

Unlike us, the man with the good word enjoys "holding his peace." He knows that "no man doth safely speak but he that is glad to hold his peace." If he appears somewhat reticent it is because he has learned that "it is easier not to speak at all than not to exceed in speech." He is slow to offer advice and counsel and he never entangles himself with things not entrusted to him. He is no busybody. He agrees with À Kempis that "it is safer to hear and take counsel than to give it."

The art, the faculty of keeping one's mouth shut is essential to a life of brotherhood and love. The tongue is "untamable"; it is "a fire," "a world of iniquity" (St. James); and often the only way to control it is to lock it in. To be able to clamp your jaws shut is a *sine qua non* of love.

"Oftentimes," cries the kindly À Kempis, "I could wish I had held my peace when I have spoken." The hard, bitter word had often, no doubt, slipped past his watchful guard.

We think that we please others by chatting away. Perhaps, sometimes, we do. More often, when we count on "pleasing others by our society, we rather displease them with those bad qualities which they discover in us" (À Kempis).

Even for our own good, we talk too much. We trust
every casual acquaintance and put ourselves in his power.
"Lay not thy heart open to everyone," warns À Kempis.
If not in charity to others, at least in charity to ourselves,
we should learn to keep our mouths shut. We might well
take to heart the moral of an epitaph, inscribed under a
glass frame containing a stuffed fish: "I wouldn't be here
if I had kept my mouth shut!"

In a life of brotherhood the maxim, "Say nothing but
good about the dead," is not sufficient. The maxim must
be, "Neither of the living nor of the dead say aught but
good."

This rule of love is hard — perhaps the hardest of all —
but it is absolutely essential. You can't be a good neighbor if you judge and say ill *of anyone*. Were we to do
no more, in the way of serving others, than to speak well
of them, we should already be splendid altruists and social
workers. "If any man offend not in word, the same is a
perfect man" (St. James).

Trouble starts when we allow ourselves to criticize and
judge others. We have no right to judge others; to do so
is always wrong as well as foolish. "In judging others a
man laboreth in vain, often erreth, and easily sinneth;
but in judging and examining himself, he always laboreth
fruitfully" (À Kempis).

We have neither the right nor the ability nor the
freedom from prejudice that just judgments demand.
"We judge things according as we fancy them, for private
affection bereaves us easily of a right judgment." (À Kempis). We weigh ourselves and what we do on one scale,

tipping it in our own favor. When we weigh our neighbor and his conduct, we tip the scale in his disfavor; or we use a scale that cheats. "How seldom we weigh our neighbor in the same balance with ourselves!"

If a neighbor neglects to pay us what he owes, it is, we say, because he is trying to get out of paying, to rob us. If we fail to pay what we owe, it is not due to any dishonest intention, but to mere forgetfulness!

We find fault with others because they do not live up to a high standard of perfection. Why? Do we not know, from experience, how difficult it is to do things right? "If," says À Kempis, "thou canst not make thyself such an one as thou wouldst, how canst thou expect to have another in all things to thy liking?"

The man with the good word avoids judging others, for he sees the evil it leads to and the folly of it. He minds his own business. He prefers to think well of others and to think ill of himself, rather than to scrutinize the faults of others. This is great wisdom. "It is great wisdom and perfection to think nothing of ourselves, and to think, always, well and highly of others" (À Kempis).

Life, the true life of peace and friendship for all, begins then, and not any sooner, when we abandon the miserable habit of criticizing, judging, *and, as a consequence, hating our brothers.*

No one can understand fully the secret of human misery and suffering until he understands the part the tongue takes in the economy of social life. The tongue, though "a little member, boasteth great things." It does incalculable harm. It creates and spreads hate and ruin.

The unbridled tongue is Public Enemy No. 1. Whether in a club or in an office, in a family circle or in a convent or monastery, wherever it appears, it "defiles" and "inflames." It is the enemy of religion and of good will. "If any man think himself to be religious, not bridling his tongue . . . this man's religion is vain." We can turn St. James's words to read: "If any man think himself to be social-minded and altruistic, not bridling his tongue . . . this man's philanthropy is vain."

The reason the unbridled tongue is Public Enemy No. 1 is because it creates and breeds hate.

Every politician, every businessman, every clergyman, every nun in her convent, every girl at college, every child at home knows that it is the bitter word of jealousy, envy, or mere spite that sets ill will and enmity afire. Among nations, as among classes and religions, libelous statements always engender fury. Until leaders, as well as little folk, learn to use the good word instead of the evil word, the world will continue full of hate.

We bewail the fact that there is too much hate in the world, and we grieve because of the sorrow and misery that hate entails. But our lamentation and sorrow over the existence of hate is hypocritical, so long as we maintain enmities and dislikes in our own hearts, so long as we suffer the evil word to cross our lips.

To fight hate we must acquire the use of the good word until it becomes second nature to us. The man who has the good word on his lips (whatever the situation may be), is illustrated by the person in a group that is gathered around a dead rat and gazing at it. While others express disgust in loud "Ugh's!" he murmurs: "What lovely teeth!"

Through articles and books on popular psychology everyone knows of the ill effects of the emotion of hate on both the body and the mind. Hate disfigures you and makes you ill. The man with hate in his heart — I speak of intense, consuming hate — is restless, moody, and his face assumes repulsive lines. His glands no longer function normally. He is tense; his sleep suffers. He finds no joy in the ordinary affairs of life. His passion enchains him; his moral stature sinks; he inspires neither love nor trust. He is like a self-confessed *murderer*. St. John calls him such: "He who hates his brother is a murderer."

Even though our hates be less intense, less absorbing; even though they be *only* antipathies and dislikes, they still injure us mentally and physically, and nature's sanction for the law of love exacts its toll of us.

Our enmities depress us and rob us of peace. Whatever charm and gaiety we normally possess disappear. Even a *little* hate makes us ugly and repulsive.

What are we to do about hate? How are we to escape from it?

If the cause of our hating someone is objective, namely, a wrong done us, there is no alternative to the cure recommended to us by Christ, the Good Physician. We must forgive our enemy. *We must forgive freely, readily, and wholeheartedly.* "Be ye kind to one another; merciful, forgiving one another, even as God hath forgiven you in Christ" (St. Paul). When we forgive generously we begin to love instead of hate the one who wronged us. Great peace then will be ours.

If the cause of our hate is subjective and due to jealousy on our part, or to touchiness, escape from hate is easier. We may not escape from our blameworthy hate by force of reasoning; the antipathy may still remain. But once we begin, sincerely, to do good to those for whom we feel a great dislike, we are on the road to success. We must use the good word in our dealings with them, and in their absence speak nothing but good of them. Our antipathy and dislike will not long survive this strategy.

There was a girl once who used to go out walking, alone, and talking aloud to herself. People noticed her and thought that she was "going queer" in the head. But she was really a sensible, though very shy, girl. When she was asked what she was up to, she answered: "I can't say a word in company, so I go out talking to myself, *to get accustomed to talking to people.*"

The girl had a great idea! In some such way some of us could acquire the habit of employing the good word.

It is unfortunately part of our fallen nature to be prone to hate, rather than prone to love. We are always fully prepared with sharp retorts to meet attacks. We expect them. We await onsets of hate. We are on our toes to hate right back. This attitude is what lies behind our readiness to take offense.

One day in a bus two ladies sat on opposite sides appraising one another.

One suddenly leaned over and remarked: "Ma'am, your hat is crooked!"

The second lady was ready. In her turn she leaned forward to say: "Ma'am, there's a smudge on your nose!"

No doubt, these two ladies thereafter hated one another.

Why didn't the first lady keep her mouth shut and mind her own business? How wise the remark of À Kempis, quoted above: "It is safer to hear and take counsel than to give it"!

Life begins with love. It begins with good will toward all, that expresses itself in serving and helping others, with humility and deep sincerity. It is sustained by "thinking, always, well and highly of others," and speaking the good word of everyone. It means great peace of mind, great inner happiness. It means the satisfaction of leading a useful, worth-while life. "He does much who loves much . . . he is truly great who hath great love."

Chapter 9

THOUGHTFULNESS

You begin to live; in a sense, you begin to live two lives when you are thoughtful about the needs of others. You live a worth-while life of your own, and you share in the life of the person you are concerned about.

That person has a headache, perhaps, and you avoid making noise and fussing around. He says, though you can't hear him: "Thank goodness for the quiet!"

The family car needs washing and you have time to do the job. The next member of the family who drives the car, spotless and shiny, out of the garage, will be delighted. In some way you get a bit of that delight.

Someone you know gets a good job or passes an exam or is elected to some important post. You look up his telephone number and tell him how glad you are over his success. The happiness he finds in your friendly gesture radiates into you.

St. Paul, always graphic and forceful, tells us the secret of thoughtfulness when he says that we should put ourselves, in imagination, into the shoes (or shackles) of other people. "Remember them that are in bonds," he says, "as if you were bound with them; and them that labor as being yourself also in the body."

When I was about five years of age I had a cat called Button, a motherly cat, a great pal.

One day I fell ill and Button came to sleep at the foot of my bed. She seemed to be concerned about me.

I grew a bit worse and Button noticed something was wrong with my breathing. Dogs and cats are, I think, quick to sense irregularity in the breathing of humans.

Anyhow, when Button noticed my breathing wasn't right she left the room and was away for a while. When she returned she had a mouse in her mouth — a nice little mouse, one would call it. She crept up to my pillow and left the mouse beside my head for me to eat!

Then she retired to the foot of the bed to watch how I enjoyed the dinner she provided, and, no doubt, to see if it did me good. Though only a cat, she gave me quite a lesson in thoughtfulness.

The scope of thoughtfulness embraces all those minor human contacts that make up our social lives. About 95 per cent of our relations with others have to do with non-momentous things. We meet and greet friends and neighbors; we eat, chat, and work with people, mostly the same people, every day. We can go through these humdrum contacts in a dull, mechanical way or we can go through them with imagination and sympathy. Our life can be full or it can remain empty according to the measure of our thoughtfulness. If we are ever on the lookout for opportunities to increase the happiness of others we can make our world a much better place to live in. It is, as we said already, easy to make others happier, and that through little things.

Thoughtfulness is easy to cultivate and easy to develop. It does not demand much effort, and usually there is no sacrifice involved. All that it calls for is the use of our imagination. It adds great charm, great attractiveness, to our personality. It is the essense of civilized living; it is courtesy in the best sense.

If you are thoughtful you will not retain for long a book or other article, from a binocular to a garden tool, that has been loaned to you. You take it for granted that the owner wants the object back. If you are thoughtful you answer promptly letters that call for a reply, and write as often as you can to those who long to hear from you. A letter to those who love you can afford incredible joy. If you are thoughtful you will inquire after those who are sick, and visit them if you are sure that your visit will give pleasure. If you are thoughtful you will cut out grumbling and complaining at home and in your office, for who does not know how disagreeable it is to have to listen to complaints?

To keep in mind the needs of others, their real, urgent needs, is the characteristic of the thoughtful person. In this respect we have a very touching example given in the Gospel.

The scene was the bedroom in the home of Jairus, the Jewish ruler, where Christ called back to life Jairus' daughter. The girl, twelve years of age, weak and frail after her illness, arose from her deathbed as Christ took her hand.

All present were struck with wonder at the miracle and then their wonder turned into joy. They crowded around congratulating the girl's parents and, no doubt, hugging and kissing the girl and asking her a lot of questions. Full of excitement and thrilled by their experience, the people thought of everything but of what the poor girl really needed. It was Christ alone who thought of *that*. He realized how weak and hungry this twelve-year-old girl was and "He ordered that food should be given to her." How glad she must have been to hear that word *food!*

Thoughtfulness becomes a habitual attitude of mind and heart that grows sensitive and many-sided. It shows itself in every phase of living. The thoughtful man gives others the right of way in traffic when he sees their difficulties; he avoids, as far as possible, tooting the horn; he obeys all traffic regulations; he is a courteous driver. At table he is attentive to the wants of others, restraining, for the sake of others, his hurry to get food. In a restaurant or in a store he does not insist noisily on his rights, whatever they may be, but patiently makes allowance for overworked or flustered waiters or clerks. Always he puts himself in the place of others, through his sympathetic imagination, and acts decently.

It is in a home, among the family, that thoughtfulness is needed most of all. Parents need to think wisely and well and to put first things first. Children *need* good food, and plenty of room to sleep and play, rather than expensive cars and exotic furniture. If family resources are limited, the first call on them should be for plenty of living space and the best of food. Children *need* a home that is a *home*, namely, where their parents are. And thoughtful parents stay home most evenings to be with their children, and they interest themselves in their children's interests. They aim to create a happy community spirit, one of love, cheerfulness, and co-operation. In a home where mutual trust prevails; where burdens are shared by all; where honor and respect are shown to all; where rancor and quarrels are avoided; where each feels sympathy and compassion for each; and where "one gives to him that asketh and from him that would borrow turns not away," you find the triumph of parental thoughtfulness — a triumph that is well worth while.

Children will not be thoughtful unless they learn the lesson from their parents. They will not consider their parents' needs and wishes unless they have acquired sympathetic imagination. They will not enjoy spending evenings at home unless they see a "home spirit" in their parents. But when they do come to love home life they make their parents happy. What father is not thrilled when he hears his son say: "Dad, is there anything you want me to do?" What mother is not delighted when her daughter *willingly* helps her out with chores? When the members of the family occupy themselves with the needs of others the success of the home is secure.

The hallmark of a good home is hospitality, kindness, and thoughtfulness toward visitors and guests. Hospitality is not selective; it is shown to all, the poor as well as the rich, the "bore" as well as the interesting friend.

In the rules of St. Benedict we read: "All those who come [to the monastery gate] shall be received as if they were Christ in person, for He will say to us one day: 'I was a stranger and you took Me in.'" The Apostles, who in their travels experienced the need of hospitality, urge it upon us as a necessary virtue. "Pursue hospitality. . . . Be given to hospitality . . . use hospitality one towards another without murmuring," they wrote. St. Paul, who saw the mystic beauty of it, added: "And hospitality do not forget, for by this, some, not being aware of it, have entertained angels."

When a visitor comes to see us, whether at our office or in our home, no matter who he be, we should treat him with respect and in a kindly way, putting him at his ease, and making him feel that he is welcome. If we are curt, cold, or arrogant — if we show him that we are bored — we fail miserably. He may have a request to make, or he may have dropped in for a chat; whatever his purpose in calling on us, we should place ourselves at his service.

If there is occasion to entertain a guest, we should be sincere and generous in our hospitality, offering the best we have to offer. To entertain with a view to a return is not hospitality but trading. To entertain so as to share our possessions and our friendship with a brother; so as to make him happy, and that without murmuring over the trouble or expense, is apostolic hospitality, the kind we are bidden, as Christians, to practice. Such hospitality brings a blessing on a home, and is a splendid lesson for young members of the family.

The first claims on our thoughtfulness are the claims of those who are near and dear to us, who have won our love, to whom we are indebted. Our parents, our relations, our old friends, our teachers, servants, or nurses who watched over us when we were young, kind neighbors of early days.

About these we should ask ourselves: "What do they expect of us?" And we should keep in mind that indifference and neglect on our part may cause deep hurt and sorrow. It does not cost much to send a token of remembrance from time to time to those to whom we owe what is best in life.

Honor is involved in facing and paying our debts of gratitude. Others, who have helped us, have rights to our attention and consideration, rights that should be respected. It is the part of an honorable man to acknowledge such rights.

Take the case of an old nurse, living alone and far from the family of which she was once a valued and faithful member. Are not her thoughts constantly turned toward those she helped to rear? What if they completely forget her?

I knew a young professional man who made it a point, every month or so, to travel quite a long way to visit his old nurse and stay a couple of hours to chat with her. Often he would bring her presents, and take her for a drive in his car. When she died he assumed the responsibility of burying her in a splendid and befitting manner.

I know men, no longer young, who still visit and write to their old teachers in order to make them happier in their old age, by reason of being remembered. The claim of an old teacher on his pupils is not in any sense a claim of strict justice, but nonetheless it is a real claim.

It is a precious thing to have a few friends and to keep them for sake of the bond of sympathy and fellowship. Friendship grows richer and mellower with the passing of years but it is a delicate wine that needs careful keeping. It is on the basis of thoughtful conduct that friendship survives.

If trouble or misfortune crosses my path, what do I expect of my friend? If trouble crosses his path what does he expect of me? Will I say the word, or write the letter, or give the aid that will comfort him? Am I thoughtful? Tactful? Will I meet the claim of honor?

In their old age many parents are morose, complaining, niggardly. They expect too much from their children; the wisdom and patience that becomes gray hairs and stiffening joints is lacking. They no longer inspire emotional love or admiration. None the less their just claims on their children should be met. Children should always show them respect and honor. They should strive to give them moments of happiness. They should never turn their backs on them and abandon them.

If we are thoughtful we will keep our ears open to the just complaints of others. If we do so we will hear about the things in us that hurt and annoy others; about our rudenesses and selfish ways; about our injustices and cruelties.

A married man may not realize how terribly his unpunctuality, or his proneness to gamble, makes his wife suffer. He does not see his conduct as it appears in her eyes; *he does not think!* He is, we suppose, devoted to his wife and concerned about her happiness, and about their mutual interests. Her claim that he should change his ways is well founded. If he is honorable he will meet that claim. To do so is thoughtfulness!

The alibi of the thoughtless person is the word *forget*. Mother's day comes around and he *forgets* to send his mother a message or a present. He leaves home for the day and he *forgets* to fill a bowl of water for his dog. A friend is sick in a hospital and he *forgets* to visit him. Someone has a sore arm and he brushes against it. Always he *forgets*.

If the claims and rights of others meant anything to him he would not forget; he would remember them as well as he remembers his own rights and claims. The trouble with the thoughtless person does not lie in his memory, but in his heart.

It's not enough to be thoughtful of one or two people whom we understand and love very much; we have to be considerate of everyone. We have to keep reminding ourselves that everyone whom we know and meet wants to be treated with respect by us, and appreciates kindness. When we think of another with respect — honoring him in our minds — we are pretty sure to be thoughtful in his regard.

In the long run it is love that counts above everything else. The Christian love with which a good deed is performed enhances its value — and makes it immortal. A good deed done for Christ and in a Christ-like way has an effect that it is impossible to estimate. Such a deed "goes around and around"; its ramifications are incalculable; it leads to other good deeds; it affects permanently the recipient and those that know about it. Magdalen's act of love and courtesy to Christ, when she anointed His feet, will be known to the end of time, wherever the Gospel is preached. Other acts of love and courtesy paid to Christ's "substitutes," having the same value, partake of the same quality of immortality. It is surely worth while to be thoughtful.

Chapter 10

HELPFULNESS

The *helpful* person is ready to lend a hand, any time, anywhere. He is at your service "not with sadness of necessity," but "with simplicity" and "with cheerfulness" (St. Paul). If you are looking for something he joins in the search or says: "I think I've got what you want." If you are in a hurry to finish a task and ask his assistance, he doesn't say: "I'll be over as soon as I get this job done." He comes right away, leaving his own task to complete later. Like a dog that wags his tail and is off when he hears a whistle, the helpful person is happy to be at the call of everyone.

Often in a community or club or home there is someone who voluntarily takes care of the little odd jobs that require attention. The things to fix, to replace, to arrange — things that are really everybody's business — are looked after by him or her. But for this obliging, devoted person things would not run smoothly. Once in a while you say to such a one: "I don't know what we'd do without you!" The helpful person is the servant of all; the source of kindness and love. Often we feel ashamed at our selfishness and laziness when we observe how much goodhearted people do for the common happiness.

To be helpful money is not necessary, nor brains, nor beauty — only love, love of neighbor. The prompt willingness to help, the ready spirit, and the purpose of mind spring from love. Helpfulness lingers on into old age, and among those who are feeble and fading, there are still some who "do not forget to do good and to impart" (St. Paul). Once acquired, the habit of helpfulness never dies — it preserves the heart from growing sour.

In one of his books for the Christophers (*Careers That Change Your World,* p. 258), Father James Keller tells about a young man who, on a bed of pain, turned his mind away from his own suffering, and vowed to spend his life helping others in distress. When he recovered his health he advanced far in the field of social work which he chose as his profession in observance of his vow. "I feel now as I did then" (when on his bed of pain), he will tell you. "If I help just one person a day, by the time I'm an old man I'll have helped thousands. It's the least I can do for all that God has done for me."

The helpful act that you perform may seem trivial. "Easy and nothing to it!" you say; but to the person helped it may be extremely important. You may be saving a life by such a petty service as holding the reins of a restive horse when a man is mounting, or by carrying a heavy parcel for an old person struggling up a hill. You fetch a glass of water for someone who faints; you write a letter for someone who is illiterate; you supply a man who is fishing by your side on a wharf with bait when he has exhausted his own stock; whatever the tiny act whereby you help a neighbor, its effect on the other, if done with kindliness, and for Christ's sake, is great and enduring.

Dr. Albert Schweitzer, out of his vast experience, was deeply impressed by a small courtesy he witnessed in a railway car in Germany. With him in the car were an old countryman and a student. The train was approaching a large city and it was growing dark. The old man was very agitated. He told aloud how he had received a telegram to say that his son was dying in a hospital in the city they were nearing. He wanted terribly to see his son before he died. "But," said the old fellow, "I don't know how I'll find the hospital in the dark in this big city. I'm from the country, and I'll lose my way, and my son will die before I can get to him."

Then the young student spoke up: "I know the city well, Mister. I'll get out of the train with you and bring you to the hospital. Then I'll catch another train and continue my journey."

How attractive — how *real* — such an act of helpfulness is!

At one time or another most of us find ourselves in dire need of the assistance of another. On such occasions, if the assistance is forthcoming, we realize the deep significance of brotherhood.

One of my experiences of "dire need" was in the cold, choppy sea that surrounds the granite headland of Bri Chualain, to the south of Dublin.

My brother and I had decided to swim around part of this headland. We were boys of fourteen and sixteen, he being elder, and a better swimmer than I.

The day was cold and windy as we set out alone. It was just a boys' adventure; it wasn't carefully planned. At first all went well, but as we proceeded I found the going hard — the cold was terrible. It was a longer swim, too, than I had thought.

When we were about three quarters of the way around, my strength began to give out and I was numb. My strokes were becoming faster and shorter. I began to grow anxious. Then my brother, noticing that I was tiring, swam up close to me and began talking. It was encouraging to hear him "kid me along." His near presence, too, was new strength. I knew he would stand by me if I failed completely.

I struggled on and on and at last my feet touched the stones on the shore. Then I stumbled out, frozen and exhausted.

We had left our clothes on the bank but I was unable to put mine on. My brother wrapped his coat around me and carried me to a near-by tavern where one could get hot coffee. I still remember the concern in his young voice when he told the tavern man: "Put brandy in it!" He watched while I drank the coffee until some color returned to my face. For me that long-past adventure was an experience of "help in need" that taught me what a good heart does.

The two phases of love, thoughtfulness and helpfulness, go hand in hand and supplement each other. Thoughtfulness is incomplete without helpfulness; and helpfulness is liable to run into error, through over-enthusiasm, without thoughtfulness.

The person who is, as it were, *overready* to help is liable to interfere where he is not needed. There is, in the field of helping others, an equilibrium to be established. While we should be "on our toes," ready to jump to the aid of others, we should be humble and realize that there are situations where harm rather than good is done by our overeagerness to help. Interfering in other people's affairs can work havoc.

Not all of us are qualified "trouble shooters." As a boy I got a sharp lesson in the matter of trouble shooting. I got the lesson in a railway terminal. I meant well — but it is not enough to mean well — I overestimated my smartness.

The railway platform was crowded when I noticed a man prone on the ground — as I thought, overcome by weakness — unconscious. He was a very big fellow and breathing heavily.

A few feet away, under a pillar, I observed a bucket full of water. I recognized myself as the hero of the situation and, thinking to cure the man of his spell, I laid hold of the bucket of water and emptied the contents on the head of the prone giant.

I had made a mistake. I saw it at once.

The man sprang up and began to attack the people nearest to him. He went after them, one by one, throwing them down. The neighbor in distress to whose assistance I had come had gone berserk!

I ran away as fast as I could. There was no further room for another "good deed" from me.

As a near riot developed a half dozen stalwart redcaps

arrived on the scene and the infuriated drunk was over-powered and led away.

"Be not wise in your own conceits," St. Paul has said, but I had not learned that lesson at the time.

When people are sick is a time for lending assistance (when and where needed), but it is not the time for amateur physicians to prescribe remedies. Love in the human heart does not imply an infused knowledge of medicine. It is a sad fact that kindness sometimes kills when it is divorced from thoughtfulness.

I had a friend, a learned man but unendowed with money, who suffered from a serious heart ailment. A bad spell came and he was confined to bed. Neighbors, among others a retired railroad linesman, used to come in to help. The linesman, Mike, a well-meaning old fellow, had learned to cook in his early days — and he had invented a fabulous dish that he called "railwayman's stew."

One day I was with my friend as he lay abed when Mike arrived with a steaming pot of greasy stew. He knew my friend had had little to eat and he insisted upon his eating a plate of the stew, promising him that it would do him a world of good.

My friend ate the stew. That night, poor fellow, he died.

Let's help, and be ready to help, everyone, everywhere, but let's be cautious and humble in offering service or remedies. Let's not be too confident in our own opinion. To quote again from À Kempis: "I have often heard that it is safer to hear and to take counsel than to give it."

It sometimes happens that the very best means at our disposal of helping people is to get out of their way.

Who has not had the experience of entering the domain of a busy cook with the idea of lending a hand and being told, quite bluntly, "If you want to help me, get out of my kitchen!"

Who does not know of self-appointed entertainers at parties who insist on helping with the fun, but who in reality would help things much more by keeping quiet?

Love has negative as well as positive duties, and the chief negative duty is to avoid embarrassing or inconveniencing our neighbors by our vain and selfish antics. *Love implies self-effacement.*

If you bore someone, you are *helping* that person by ceasing to bore him. When you are sick and overinsistent on attentions, constantly ringing the bell at your bedside, when you are a bother to others, you have the opportunity of helping by curbing your requirements. St. Paul, lest he should be a charge on others, supported himself by the work of his own hands. He who was so ready to carry the burdens of others, took care to help them by being no burden to them.

The boy at college who pays his own expenses by taking jobs and working his way, helps his parents at home. The girl who makes her own things to spare her father's pocketbook is likewise a loving helper.

To endure for love's sake is part of the better life, "the excellent way."

Chapter 11

EXEMPLARS OF BROTHERHOOD:
PETER AND PAUL

SOME readers may still wonder what is meant by saying that "life begins with love." Often an example makes a concept clearer; often, too, it stands as a kind of proof of a doctrine.

The example that I offer of the doctrine that life begins with love, lies in the "rebirth" of Peter and Paul which followed their learning from Christ the meaning and the practice of love of their fellow men.

Peter, as everyone knows, was, in his early days, an impulsive, vain fellow. He was boastful but easily frightened, and when frightened, he became a coward. At times he was sulky and interfering. He was prone to violence. He showed no signs of pity or compassion for others. He was, we may say, an average, rough, selfish fisherman.

Paul was even more asocial than Peter. He was a cocksure, angry, conceited fellow, learned to be sure, but bitter. He was a cruel, intolerant partisan; a very dreadful man to have as an enemy. He seems to have been quite bereft of pity or good will.

No doubt, both Peter and Paul had, latent within them, loyalty, strength of character, and noble instincts. But

84

the lives they lived before love took possession of their hearts were in no way noble or kindly.

We wonder why Christ chose two such men as instruments wherewith to govern and found His Church; we wonder, that is, until we remind ourselves that Christ knew the vast change divine and human love would bring about in them. What was this change? What did love do for them?

It is not our purpose to study the changes wrought in their souls alone, but rather *in their humanity,* in their characters as humans. We know that spiritually they grew so close to Christ that "Christ lived in them," and they in Christ, and that they were sanctified as few humans have been sanctified.

It is our purpose to remark on the new lives they led, lives full of energetic action for the moral and material good of their fellow men; lives full of kindness and courtesy and affection. The new Peter was to become a brave, benevolent, generous leader; the new Paul was to become the wisest, lovingest man that ever wore himself out in the service of others.

Let us glance first at the new life of the new Peter, the Peter transmorphized by love.

When Peter took over the reins of government of the Church, its members were, for the most part, poor and in sore distress. Solicitous for their welfare, he organized relief centers. He taught the rich to sell out their belongings and "give to the poor." They obeyed his wishes. "Their possessions and goods they sold and divided them to all." Men and women, followers of Christ, "broke bread from house to house," and "took their meat with gladness and simplicity of heart." Peter organized so well that "neither was there any needy among them," for "distribution was made to everyone according as he had need." Peter himself passed around the bread and fish and wine at the tables until the institution of the deacons took up this work. Peter was now thinking about others, caring for others, *an exemplar of thoughtfulness and helpfulness.*

Peter had to consecrate other bishops. He chose the best and most reliable men available. But some were perhaps severe, and some young and inexperienced. He had to instruct them in the way of brotherhood. "Feed the flock of God which is among you," he told them, "taking care of it not by constraint, but willingly according to God; not for filthy lucre's sake, but voluntarily; neither as lording it over the clergy but being made a pattern to the flock from the heart." Peter wanted the rule of love in the Church. Knowing the cleansing influence of love he warned all his followers to "purify their souls in the obedience of charity." What a change from the violent man who had drawn a sword in the garden to strike off the ear of one of Christ's assailants!

As the fame of Peter's goodness of heart spread among the people, "they brought forth the sick into the streets, and laid them on beds and couches, that when Peter came his shadow at the least might overshadow any of them and they might be delivered from their infirmities."

There are in the accounts of Peter's miracles, as recorded in the Gospels, details which indicate his great courtesy and gentleness. In the miracle at the Gate Beautiful, when the lame man was healed, Peter "took him by the hand" and lifted him to his feet, as though to reassure him in an affectionate and familiar way. In the miracle when he raised Tabitha to life he took her by the hand, "and when he had called the saints and widows he presented her alive." There was kindness and charm in the way he did things.

It was no wonder that women liked and trusted him. They knew he understood their feelings, busy bishop though he was. They felt they could "get things out of him," as it were. See them, for example, *before* he called back Tabitha from death. "All the widows stood about him, weeping and showing him the coats and garments which Tabitha had made." Peter was the kind of bishop they wanted; one full of sympathy and compassion.

It is customary to regard tolerance as an important criterion of brotherhood and love. The tolerance of Peter survived the severest tests. He was the first, after Christ, to defend his fellow countrymen, the Jews, from the charge of being "Christ-killers." "I know that you did it in ignorance," he told them. Though more cautious than Paul, Peter was a pioneer in liberalizing the conditions for accepting pagan Gentiles into the Church. He accepted an invitation from Cornelius, a Roman officer, to enter his house and eat with him. "You know," said Peter on entering, "how abominable a thing it is for a man who is a Jew to keep company or to come unto one of another nation; but God hath showed me to call no man common or unclean. For which cause, making no doubt, I came when I was sent for." Then, having heard Cornelius' remarkable story, Peter went on: "In very deed I perceive that God is not a respecter of persons. *But in every nation, he that feareth him and worketh justice, is acceptable to him.*"

In these words of the first Pope we have the germ of the wonderful liberality of the Church's doctrine concerning the salvation of those who are "technically" outside the Church.

The only three words comparable to Christ's three words, "Love thy neighbor," were coined and taught and practiced by Peter. They are: "Honor all men!" Peter's rule is an incomparable paraphrase of Christ's. It expresses the acme of love for one's fellow man. It could only spring out of a heart that was "right" through and through. Further, Peter tells us "to have compassion one for another"; and reaching into the secret of brotherhood, he warns us "to insinuate humility one to another."

Peter was a big man, often very hungry, very tired, and very sleepy. He had to travel a great deal and to depend on hospitality. He came to appreciate the value and significance of hospitality and he wanted Christians to be hospitable. He taught us thus: "Use hospitality one toward another without murmuring." How well the rough old fisherman had progressed in the niceties of charity since love entered his heart! This, indeed, is a "new" Peter, living a "new" life!

In his ever-growing gentleness, Peter was not afraid to be emotional about neighborliness. He told us, "with a brotherly love, from a sincere heart, to love one another earnestly." Never should we "render evil for evil, or railing for railing, but contrariwise blessing." He kept on teaching and repeating his doctrine of love and even wrote a last Epistle, shortly before his martyrdom, "to put you all in remembrance of these things, though indeed you know them." To the very end, this great human-hearted leader kept in touch with his followers, thinking of them and caring for them — and dying that they might be saved in Christ.

Before the great change came over Paul, before love entered his heart and his "new" life began, we find him "breathing threats and slaughter" against Christians. There was a mighty hate in his heart then, and his mind stank with pride.

When the change came and the new Paul spoke, his voice carried this message: "The love of our neighbor worketh no evil. . . . Be ye kind one to another, merciful, forgiving one another even as God hath forgiven you in Christ." The new Paul no longer persecutes his fellow men. He comforts, consoles, encourages others; he collects alms for the poor; he supports terrified soldiers and sailors in a storm; he saves an unfortunate jailer from committing suicide; he writes a marvelous letter to protect a runaway slave from being whipped. Meanwhile, lest he be a charge on others, while he preaches to them and teaches them, he supports himself by the labor of his hands. He is no longer a haughty Pharisee and doctor of law, but a simple friendly little bishop who is "all things to all men." He carries on his shoulders the burdens of others and bids us do likewise. "Bear one another's burdens; and so you will fulfill the law of Christ."

The new Paul is deeply and sincerely solicitous about his friends, as, for instance, about Timothy and his "frequent infirmities." He urges Timothy, thoughtfully, "Do not still drink water but take a little wine." When Zenas and Apollo are to make the journey to visit him, he orders: "Let nothing be wanting to them." In the case of Epaphroditus, "his brother, fellow-laborer, and fellow-soldier," he calls on the Philippians to show him special honor, "because for the work of Christ he came to the point of death." He was beloved for his fidelity, for his generosity, for his courage and his faith. His parting from his Ephesian friends shows how he was loved. "And there was much weeping among them all; and falling on the neck of Paul they kissed him, being grieved most of all for the word which he had said, that they should see his face no more."

Where is the hate? Where is the pride that dominated the erstwhile Paul? Where is the intolerance?

Now Paul loves all men equally. "There is," he says, "neither Gentile nor Jew, circumcision nor uncircumcision, Barbarian nor Scythian, bond nor free, but Christ is all and in all." Now, instead of being a persecutor and murderer, he can boast: "I am clear from the blood of all men."

Paul in his universal charity thinks of everybody and of every class, old and young, sinners and slaves, robbers, husbands, wives, and children. He has advice and precepts for all, "each one not considering the things that are his own, but those that are other men's." He thinks of workers and says: "Masters, do to your servants that which is just and equal, knowing that you also have a master in heaven." He thinks of the old and says: "Rebuke not old men"; he thinks of wives and says to husbands: "Be not bitter toward your wives"; he thinks of children and says to parents: "Provoke not your children lest they be discouraged." He thinks of sinners and bids us "forgive and comfort" them, "lest they be swallowed up with overmuch grief."

Love changed Paul's life, renewed it, enhanced it, until he, once ruthless and proud, became the most humble and lovable of men. Once he took to the road of brotherhood he never faltered. He kept faith with love and justly boasted: *"Fidem servavi* – I kept the faith." He verified Christ's prophecy – and learned its meaning by practice: "It is a more blessed thing to give than to receive."

To Peter and Paul, the Church, in their Octave Mass, applies words from the Book of Wisdom: "These are men of mercy whose goodly deeds have not failed" (*Hi viri misericordiae sunt, quorum pietates non defuerunt*). To these inspired words we humbly add: Their lives began with love!

Chapter 12

LOVE FOR THE MANY

It BELONGS to brotherhood to have compassion not only for the individual but for the many.

This kind of love — love for the many — calls for rare goodness of heart, for a more enlightened charity, than does love for the individual. It is comparatively easy to feel keen sympathy for a wounded man or a hungry beggar, but it is not so common to feel a like or even greater sympathy for a famine-stricken people. And of course it is not always possible to do anything effective in the latter case.

There are millions of radio listeners who are deeply moved when they hear eye-witness accounts of a group of men working frantically and heroically against time to save a child who has fallen into a deep well. The same millions hear with comparative indifference that a volcanic eruption in New Guinea has caused thousands of fatalities. Clearly the minds and hearts of these millions have not the attitude that brotherhood calls for. The larger the scale of the suffering, the less they seem to care.

Christ taught us by His example to feel compassion for the many, the multitude. He wept over the city of Jerusalem, as He foresaw its oncoming destruction. On

two occasions, when a great crowd of thousands that
had followed Him was hungry and in danger of suffering,
He supplied them with a plentiful meal. He showed us
that the way of true love is to do what we can for the
many as well as for the one. The truly kind man must
have "wisdom and understanding exceeding much, and
largeness of heart as the sand that is on the seashore"
(3 Kings 4:29).

There are great groups and classes of sufferers: victims
of polio, victims of cancer, victims of tuberculosis, displaced
persons, famine-stricken tribes and peoples, the fugitives
in Korea, lepers, slum dwellers, inmates of prisons, the
illiterate, the benighted pagans in far-off islands and con-
tinents, drug addicts, the "exploited" mass in every country. It seems as though a new group of sufferers is called
to public attention almost every day. The world is full
of spectacles of misery. "Largeness of heart as the sand
that is on the seashore" is needed that we may compassionate all stricken humans.

The task of educating ourselves to be concerned about
the many, though they be far-off and inaccessible to us,
is one we must face. The heart grows by study and by
effort. The heart is made to love and there is no limit to
its capacity. We cannot shed tears for all who are in
trouble, but we must not be indifferent or harden our
hearts toward them. As little and comparatively helpless
people, we cannot do much, we are powerless to do big
things, to undertake large-scale operations, but we can
often give a little aid. We can contribute our mite to the
Red Cross, the March of Dimes; we can send a toy or

an old coat to Europe; we can write our Congressional representative to urge that surplus food be sent to famine areas; we can solicit aid from the forgetful rich for worthy causes; we can keep active in various minor ways in the war to relieve suffering and ill. We should at least *listen* to every distant cry for help and *pray* if there is nothing our hand can do.

By reading good books that espouse worthy causes we educate ourselves and prepare ourselves for facing our social duties. Hard men keep their ears shut and their eyes closed; we must not imitate them. In the past century, when debtors' prisons and workhouses were a scandal in England, the novels of Charles Dickens paved the way for reform by painting lurid pictures of misery. People read his books, and went to the polls in a successful effort to have conditions bettered. In this country too the public has learned from good books to insist on reforms.

Intelligent brotherhood, that embraces love for the many, implies good citizenship; it implies activity in civic and national affairs; it implies active interest in having good laws enacted, and in the choice of a good government. A good citizen loves his country and obeys the laws, for in so doing he is helping others. He stands with those who fight against graft and corruption and who fight for a fair deal for all. He recognizes that, while it is good to give an alms to a beggar, it is still better to give an alms to all the people by going to the polls. The franchise is the weapon that Providence has placed in our hands and "God wills it" that we use that weapon in the modern crusade for justice.

Love for the many can and should be a powerful motive in one's life.

The Catholic doctrine and practice in regard to Purgatory affords a very beautiful illustration of love of this kind. In purgatory *the many* are our brothers and sisters, thousands, perhaps millions of them, who have died in the friendship of God, but who have still to suffer punishment for their sins, before they are sufficiently purified to enter heaven.

Catholics, mindful of the sufferings of these "poor souls," have compassion on them and pray to God for relief for them.

The poor souls are *not* in a desperate situation. Far from it! Their ultimate salvation is assured. But, *they suffer*, perhaps very grievously, and loving hearts help them out of pity.

This Catholic doctrine and practice of coming to the aid of a great multitude who are, save for a few, quite unknown to us, who belong to every race and to creeds other than our own, is an unparalleled exercise in love for the many, a unique training for the mind and heart. Every heart trained in this holy and wonderful exercise should be apt and ready to co-operate in works of physical charity for unknown masses of sufferers in foreign lands.

When we co-operate in works of mercy for large groups, such as the victims of polio or cancer, or the displaced persons of Europe, we find ourselves working with good people of religions other than our own. When we find Good Samaritans busy in deeds of mercy we do not stop to ask them: "To what Church do you belong?" We pitch in and lend a hand at once in a spirit of love and humility. It belongs to right social thinking to support organized charities that do good work, no matter by whom they are conducted. There are Jewish and Protestant charities that Catholics should gladly support. There are Catholic charities that Jews and Protestants should support. "Christ is all and in all," and the poor and suffering are His poor and suffering, no matter what their religion may be. "I perceive," said St. Peter, "that God is not a respecter of persons. But in every nation, he that feareth him, and worketh justice, is acceptable to him."

When calamity strikes on a large scale, whether it be a flood or an earthquake or a pestilence, and when the calamity does not affect us, our first impulse is to say: "We're safe, thank God! No floods here! No earthquakes! No pestilence!"

While it is right to thank God for one's safety, it is not right to allow the cozy feeling of self-security to make us indifferent. Those who are stricken by the calamity *are* our brothers and sisters. Their woes, whether we admit it or not, *are* our woes, and we should help bear them. We should put ourselves, in imagination, in their place. We should hear their cries and, at very least, pray for them. If it is wartime, and they are among our opponents, it is not for us to pray that shells and bombs may wound and kill them, but that God may reunite all in peace.

Love for the many may find an outlet in various ways, not only in works for the relief of physical suffering, but also in works to relieve the darkness of men's minds.

Editors and writers who commit good thoughts to paper and who influence thousands of unknown humans for good are eminent examples of lovers of the many. They feed hungry minds and fight the falsehood that hurts them. The press is a constant and powerful stimulus, either for right or for wrong. It can poison or it can nourish with wholesome food. Always it is directed to the many — the multitude. While a preacher or orator reaches but a few thousand with his voice — unless it is broadcast over the radio — the press always, every day, reaches millions. And readers cannot but be influenced to some extent by what they read.

There are Catholics who, though they know the power of the press, and though they hear from time to time the exhortation of their bishops to support the Catholic press, fail to take heed. They are blind to their duty of charity to the multitude who would be helped and bettered by a really successful Catholic press. How many Catholics help to spread the circulation of Catholic papers as members of other religions help to spread the circulation of their papers?

Meanwhile Catholic editors and writers face the grave responsibility of continuing to improve the product of their hands and minds. They are fighting a winning battle because, as is evident to every thoughtful reader, the quality of the Catholic press grows better and finer as the years pass.

In the Catholic press we find a magnificent effort to succor the many, to enlighten and to console, to protect and inspire, and to unite in the love of the truth.

Here, then, is an excellent exercise in brotherhood, and a practical rule for its development, to do all you can to help the many by circulating Catholic literature.

Chapter 13

YOU ARE IMPORTANT!

THE lesson of love is to be humble, to be "meek and humble of heart." Love demands forbearance on your part, and not forbearance alone, but patience, forgiveness, and respect for all. Love calls for reticence and restraint in speech, warning you against being outspoken and self-assertive. Love bids you think of yourself as weak and frail, and tells you to think highly of others. "Take the lowest seat," it says, "and yield the best things to others." But *love does not inculcate pessimism.*

Humility is not pessimism. It is not humility to say: "I am of no importance; I can do nothing."

Faith teaches us that we are all children of God; that, although of ourselves "we can do nothing," we are instruments of God and with His aid "we can do all things."

To know that we can do all things is optimism, Christian optimism, and it implies recognition of our importance.

The greater our love, the greater our humility, the more assured we are of our importance in God's economy.

The man who thinks he is important on account of his political power, or his great wealth or high talent, is a fool. The man who thinks himself important because he is the child of God is wise. We are all important, then, and we all have important things that we can do.

People may say that the man with love in his heart, as I have described him above, is a poor, "inoffensive" type, lacking boldness and initiative. "Your *kind* man," they will tell me, "your gentle, self-effacing, courteous, soft-spoken fellow is spineless — he has no guts!" They would prefer to my man of love "the popular hero" type, who maintains his rights at all costs, who lashes wrongdoers with his bold tongue, and knocks down enemies with his brave fists.

But the man of love as I have painted him need not be uncourageous, or spineless, or lacking in guts. It takes guts to restrain greed; to keep one's mouth shut in face of provocation; and "to give to him who asks of thee, and from one who would borrow of thee not to turn away."

It takes guts to bear wrong in patience.

I have seen a gentle, pious boy, a boy conspicuous for his kindness and courtesy, take a cruel, brutal lashing at the hands of an infuriated teacher without a whimper. As the leather strap cut him again and again he made no protest and uttered no cry for mercy. True gentleness and pluck combine amazingly well.

It took guts to live as lived the humblest man I ever knew. He was a convert, a priest. A great scholar and a one-time brilliant lawyer, he never wished to play the role of a "big shot." He preferred a hidden life, where he wore out the soles of shoes tramping the roads in the service of the sick and the hungry. He lived contentedly on crusts of bread. What he could he gave to the poor. He was no "tongue-lashing," "uppercutting" hero, of course, but who would dare call him spineless?

The kind of guts that is displayed in beating and humiliating a fellow human, be he good or bad, is not, if I may use the word, "Christian guts," and I doubt if there is honor or beauty in it.

The "little man" is important, then, as well as the one endowed with rank and gifts. The little man, though he be ignorant, uncouth, lame, and blind, has still his opportunity of greatness. Granted that there is love and faith in his heart, and the purpose of doing something, the whole world needs his effort!

The little man — that is, you or I — can make the world better. The little man, to use Father James Keller's happy word, can be a Christopher — a Christ-bearer — serving his fellow man in love.

When Frederick Ozanam, the Parisian student, began small-scale social work among the poor of the French capital he had no idea of the immense, world-wide effects of his initiative. The history of the Church is, largely, a repetition of stories of little men and little women who changed the world for better.

How sound, how splendid is the Christopher idea — "Do something!" — "Light a candle!" — and lastly, "You are important!" "To be a Christ-bearer," writes Father Keller (*Careers That Change Your World,* p. 263), "is to do something. And to do it is to go into the dust and heat of the market place bearing Christ and His love and compassion to those unfortunates who need them so badly."

Often it is not necessary to go as far as the market place to find people in need of love and compassion. In the office, at your doorstep, or within your own house, there may be those who need your help.

All whose purpose it is to restore the love and truth of Christ, be they within or without the Catholic fold, are Christophers. You need not be enrolled in a league, nor pay dues to a treasurer, in order to become a Christopher. All you need is to love, in an active way, your fellow humans.

To do something, rather than to criticize and talk; "to improve rather than to disprove"; to make the world better in some way or other — such is the purpose of the Christopher, while his motive is love — the love of God. "Love of all people for the love of God should be the distinguishing characteristic of anyone who would play the role of a Christopher" (*Careers That Change Your World*, p. 32).

Those who are in "key jobs" — teachers, writers, social workers, administrators in government or in labor unions — are in points of vantage for doing Christopher work. Father Keller urges those "with love in their hearts" to take up "careers that change the world" so as to find key jobs.

A million Christophers have begun the good work and have begun to discover that "life begins with love."

The movement hinges on the idea that *the individual counts* — that *the individual is important* — granted, of course, that he is inspired with purpose.

Communists train men and women to fill key positions

so as to spread their destructive, antireligious creed. They have discovered that by holding key positions they can exercise immense influence.

In the sixteenth century the Jesuit Order placed its best men in key positions in royal courts and in universities so as to stem and turn back the tide of the Reformation.

Today the idea of the Christopher movement is to gain and hold vantage points so as to save the world through Christian love. All depends upon the individual; the humble, resolute, kindly, daring Christian, who knows he can "do all things" as an instrument in God's hands.

Our lives are greatly influenced by little things. A little thing, a most trivial act of kindness, has been an inspiration to me for forty years or more. Why it should be so I do not know; the effects of a spiritual thing are unfathomable.

The incident is almost too trivial to recount. A college student, A. R., and I were sent to visit a poor couple in an out-of-the-way slum, by our St. Vincent de Paul Conference. The couple, husband and wife, were wretchedly housed and penniless. We gave them a food ticket and came away. It was just a routine call.

A. R. was not a regular member of the Conference. He was not a "likely" St. Vincent de Paul man. He was a taciturn fellow, self-centered, I thought. He never had a penny to spend on another. But that evening A. R. did something unusual — and against the Rules of the Conference.

He got a shilling somehow and went back, alone, to

visit the couple in the slum. He had noticed that the old
man had a pipe but hadn't any tobacco. With the shilling
he bought tobacco and brought it to the old man. A. R.
never told me what he had done, but I found out later
when I paid another visit to the couple.

Why should such a little act of kindness be a catalyzer
in another's soul for forty years? What is the reason for
that "immortality" in love?

We are important because we can do things.

The housewife, the caretaker, the cashier, the bellboy,
the truck driver, the retired clerk — there are things of
moment for all to do. Things small by outward measure-
ment but possibly of incalculable greatness in God's eyes.

It is impossible here to do more than suggest a few
things that members of one profession can do. I have
chosen the teacher as an example, but all of us are teachers in some way.

The teacher — what can he do about love?

When I look back upon the moral and religious education that I received I feel that it was faulty and deficient.
I was taught to be pious and "to keep myself unspotted
from the world," but due emphasis was not laid on the
fact that "religion clean and undefiled before God and
the Father is this, to visit the fatherless and widows in
their tribulation" (James 1:27).

It is up to every teacher, lay or clerical, to make clear
to their charges that *they do not and cannot know God
unless they love, in a practical way, with real action, the
people whom they contact.* St. John makes this plain when

he says: "He that loveth not, knoweth not God, for God is charity."

My teachers did not show me *why* the Good Samaritan — the roving merchant with money, wine, and a mule — was a great saint. They did not tell me that unless I acted as he acted I would be a hypocrite (like the coldhearted priest) and no Christian.

Though my formal religious training (and to be honest, it was at the hands of religious) was at the least defective, there was one who supplied the defect. In her gentle, thoughtful way, my mother gave me practical lessons in charity and tolerance. *She knew that the young have to be taught to love.*

A very poor woman, a widow, used to come into our kitchen once in a while "for a bite and a cup of tea." Whenever she came my mother would call me, and I knew what that meant. If I hadn't a penny myself I'd borrow it and bring it to the poor widow — Mrs. Dunne was her name — and give it to her respectfully and talk to her. If I had candy I'd give that too. And later, when Mrs. Dunne fell ill, and was unable to leave her hovel, my mother encouraged me to visit her and bring her whatever I could. That was excellent training in "field work" for a kid.

My mother also taught me to be tolerant. Tolerance was not very common at the time and place, for Catholics and Protestants held aloof from one another.

The nice old lady, weak and bedridden, who lived next door to us was a Protestant — a very strict Protestant at that. But she was lonely and she loved to play a simple game of chess. My mother taught me to call to see her, every week or two, and spend an hour or so with her, playing chess. Often I had to bring roses and heliotrope with me and perhaps a few chocolates. It was a way of teaching a boy brought up as a pious Catholic that love has no frontiers.

The most daring lesson of all in tolerance that my mother taught me was in respect to a married clergyman, the Rev. "Mr." Lynch, who was in charge of the local Presbyterian church. The Rev. "Mr." Lynch was a quiet, lonely man, feeble in health, who often passed our house leaning on his wife's arm. My brothers and I knew that there was something "queer" about him; finally we learned that in reality he was a "Father" Lynch who had "turned" and abandoned his Catholic flock.

In those days in Dublin, there were many who would (and did) turn their backs on the approach of an unfaithful priest, but my mother was not one of them. She insisted that my brothers and I should be most respectful and polite toward him, and she was delighted when, on a few occasions, this "Stray Shepherd" stopped to chat with us. How well my mother had grasped and how well she taught St. Paul's lesson: "Love one another with the charity of brotherhood, with honor preventing one another."

The teacher has above everyone the opportunity to indoctrinate those under him in the science and practice of brotherhood and love. He can instill into the minds of his pupils the right outlook on life and awaken their ambition to distinguish themselves in works of love. He can dare to teach — and prove — that only they who love greatly are truly great.

The teacher has to devise some form of field work in charity for his pupils and to praise and encourage them as Paul did, always urging them "to abound the more."

Children take to works of charity with zest. They find a spiritual and a psychological tonic in it. The teacher is right in taking advantage of the warmheartedness of youth.

Love has to be taught, and boys and girls are apt to learn if they are well taught. But they have to be taught through the eyes and ears and hands as well as through the mind. They have to have personal contact, in some way or other, with suffering and want, before their hearts are deeply touched. On contacting suffering and want they carry away a picture in their minds that will chasten their native selfishness. Instinctively *they will want to do* something about it. In that "wanting to do" lies the germ of active love.

A teacher should have no difficulty in realizing his importance. If he can set even one heart afire with love of others he has already achieved an immense and incalculable work for the betterment of the world.

Chapter 14

SUMMARY: FOUR RULES OF LOVE

Most of my readers do kind and neighborly deeds and know what true love is. They know that the essence of love is service. But they know also that they could do more than they do, that their love for others is intermittent, casual. They know that acts of cruelty and hate and injustice intermingle with their good deeds. They know that they do not lead the true life, the life of love, the life devoted to making the world a better place to live in. Most of my readers would like to do more than they do, but they are probably at a loss how to begin. They need "rules," practical rules, "thumb rules," wherewith to start the new life.

In the pages of the Gospel there is a veritable galaxy of lovely and wonderful rules of Christian love, but they confuse in their abundance. They cover every phase of human conduct, from truthfulness to hospitality, from thoughtfulness to generosity. "Lie not to one another"; "use hospitality one toward another without murmuring"; "think of those who are in bonds as though you were bound with them"; "give with simplicity: communicate to the necessities of the saints."

We are told, in the Scriptures, to "bear with one another";

"to honor all men"; "to love our enemies" and "those who hate us"; "to bridle our tongues"; "to have peace with all men"; "to seek not our own but that which is another's"; "to forgive and comfort" the sinner; "to be kind one to another, merciful, forgiving one another"; "to do to our servants that which is just and equal"; not "to overreach or circumvent our brother in business"; "to avoid contentions and strivings about the law"; "not to forget to do good and to impart"; and so on. Again and again the Gospels tell us to love our neighbor so as to fulfill the law.

As Christians we need to carry all these rules in our heads and in our hearts — but are there not a few thumb rules that we can carry on our finger tips?

Our thumb rules should present the very core of the lesson of charity. They should be sound, solid, authentic, while being simple and to the point. They should be plain, blunt rules, easy to understand, easy to memorize, easy to learn or to teach. They should be few in number.

Four such rules suffice.

The four rules I am about to suggest are contained in St. Paul's famous analysis of charity (1 Cor. 13), which I quote:

"Charity is patient, is kind; charity envieth not, dealeth not perversely; is not puffed up; is not ambitious; seeketh not her own; is not provoked to anger; thinketh no evil; rejoiceth not in iniquity, but rejoiceth with the truth; beareth all things; believeth all things; hopeth all things; endureth all things. Charity never falleth away; whether prophecies shall be made void, or tongues shall cease, or knowledge shall be destroyed."

The main thoughts of the sixteen items contained in this immortal analysis of love, can be gathered under four headings:

I. *Fidelity* (implying honesty).
II. *Tolerance* (implying patience and forbearance).
III. *Avoiding judging others* (implying control of the tongue).
IV. *Warmheartedness* (implying kindness and unselfishness).

The man who is faithful, tolerant, who never judges another nor utters a bitter word, and who acts always with kindness and generosity, realizes, or comes very close to realizing, St. Paul's ideal of the man of love. If you are to be such, let these be the rules of your life:

I. Keep your promises.
II. Keep your temper.
III. Keep your mouth shut.
IV. Keep your heart warm.

Now, for the explanation of each of these four rules.

Rule I

Keep Your Promises

This rule comes first because it is the rule of honesty and fidelity. I have already devoted a chapter to it.

It is justified by St. Paul's analysis given above, when he tells us that "charity dealeth not perversely" and that "charity never falleth away."

There is no deception, no "double-mindedness," about

love. If we would be good neighbors and trustworthy friends and brothers, we must keep our promises, all of them, in all our undertakings.

When we keep our promise to another we honor him, we serve him well, we give him a fair deal, and we treat him as we would be treated ourselves.

An army officer, a Protestant, came to Father Keller (*Careers That Change Your World*, p. 10), urging him to speed up the Christopher movement, saying that "this country stands a good chance of cracking up," and giving as the reason "the moral decay that is eating into everything — corruption in high places, dishonesty, perjury, graft, immorality, breakup of home life, and disregard for ordinary decency."

How can you and I fight against this spreading evil of dishonor and dishonesty — unless by keeping our promises and giving an example of fidelity?

By keeping our promises for the love of God we save ourselves and our neighbors and our country. We spread love.

May I add a serious reflection — a reflection that should strike home and hurt? Whatever dishonesty, perjury, graft, and breakup of domestic peace there may be in our own lives is due to the fact that we have not *kept our promises*.

RULE II

Keep Your Temper

This rule comes second because it is the rule of tolerance and good relations with our neighbors.

It is through forbearance, the patient bearing with the faults and annoyances of others, that we spread the light and joy of love. Forbearance means, in essence, keeping our temper, our intemperate reactions, under control.

St. Paul, in his analysis of love, says that love "is patient ... endureth all things" and "is not provoked to anger."

To be of use to the other fellow, we must get along with him, and be uniformly affable and good-tempered. If we are hot and bad-tempered we cause quarrels and start hates. Good temper is the deadly enemy of hate.

In order then to be patient with people and with the circumstances of one's life, to make allowance for the faults and foibles of others, to avoid grumbling, to show respect for the opinions of others when we disagree with them, to be in fine a tolerant, kindly brother to all, we need to *keep our temper*.

Rule III

Keep Your Mouth Shut

This rule does not mean that one is to eschew the ordinary humdrum talking and chatting that occupies quite a large part of our time. Kindness and affability demand that we converse freely with our neighbors at home and abroad.

But the rule does require that we utter no evil word that will cause pain or anger or that amounts to a judgment delivered on another. "Charity," said St. Paul (above), "envieth not ... rejoiceth not in iniquity." The man who lets his tongue run wild takes delight in discussing the sins and scandals and stupidities of others; he "rejoiceth in evil," and he "thinketh evil."

As I have pointed out above, love means the good word, and it is by the good word that we honor all men and spread good will and understanding.

This rule is a difficult one to observe — it is the work of a lifetime to observe it perfectly — but, being as it is, a *sine qua non* of charity, we have to master it.

"He never says a bad word about anyone" is a noble tribute to a man, a clear pointer to the good man's heart. Such a quality puts a man in a key position to influence others for good; everyone trusts him.

To battle and defeat hate, to lessen the suffering and wickedness in the world, we must learn to *keep our mouths shut.*

Rule IV

Keep Your Heart Warm

By this *positive* rule we compassionate others; we are merciful, generous, helpful. It is intended to be a broad rule that covers activity on behalf of others. The warm heart is the antithesis of the cold, selfish heart.

"Charity," says St. Paul (in his analysis), "is kind. . . . Charity seeketh not her own."

When your heart is warm, you refuse no request that you can grant; you withdraw from no effort that you can make. You belong to others, always aiming to do them good, to lead them to God.

When we study the gifts we have made and our manner of giving we find that we almost invariably gave less than we could have given, and gave with less humility and grace than we might have shown.

When our hearts are not warm (and humble) our gifts hurt in the giving. "God loves a cheerful giver," not one who repines over his sacrifice.

*   *   *   *

These four blunt, homely rules summarize all I have to say about love and brotherhood. They are a brief compendium of the foregoing pages.

Were I a teacher and asked by a pupil: "What rules should I follow in order to practice brotherhood?" I should teach him these rules.

Were a man or woman, depressed over the futility of his (or her) way of life, to demand of me a solution to his (or her) problem, I should likewise teach and explain these rules.

The great Abbot Columba Marmion wrote: "Love is the source of life." In these rules we have the secret of love and a sign pointing the road to better and happier living.

The kind of love embodied in these rules, is, as I wrote in the Preface, "highest reason," surpassing the mind in insight and the will in power. It enlarges your soul and, while it heals the hearts of others, it also heals your own heart.

He who will keep these rules will attain to great love, and having great love he will be truly great.